4

Teens, Nutrition, and Dieting

Christine Wilcox

Teen Well-Being

ReferencePoint Press®

San Diego, CA

For more information, contact:
ReferencePoint Press, Inc.
PO Box 27779
San Diego, CA 92198
www.ReferencePointPress.com

Picture credits:
cover: Thinkstock Images
Maury Asseng: 31, 32, 33, 46, 47, 48, 49, 61, 62, 74, 75, 76
Thinkstock Images: 10
Depositimages: 15

LIBRARY OF CONGRESS CATALOGING-IN-PUBLICATION DATA

Wilcox, Christine.
  Teens, nutrition, and dieting / by Christine Wilcox.
    pages cm. -- (Compact research series)
  Audience: Grade 9 to 12.
  Includes bibliographical references and index.
  ISBN 978-1-60152-834-6 (hardback) -- ISBN 1-60152-834-5 (hardback) 1. Teenagers--
Nutrition--Juvenile literature. 2. Diet--Juvenile literature. 3. Health--Juvenile literature.
4. Weight loss--Juvenile literature. I. Title.
  RJ235.W55   2016
  613'.0433--dc23
                                       2015003561

Contents

Foreword

As modern civilization continues to evolve, its ability to create, store, distribute, and access information expands exponentially. The explosion of information from all media continues to increase at a phenomenal rate. By 2020 some experts predict the worldwide information base will double every seventy-three days. While access to diverse sources of information and perspectives is paramount to any democratic society, information alone cannot help people gain knowledge and understanding. Information must be organized and presented clearly and succinctly in order to be understood. The challenge in the digital age becomes not the creation of information, but how best to sort, organize, enhance, and present information.

ReferencePoint Press developed the *Compact Research* series with this challenge of the information age in mind. More than any other subject area today, researching current issues can yield vast, diverse, and unqualified information that can be intimidating and overwhelming for even the most advanced and motivated researcher. The *Compact Research* series offers a compact, relevant, intelligent, and conveniently organized collection of information covering a variety of current topics ranging from illegal immigration and deforestation to diseases such as anorexia and meningitis.

The series focuses on three types of information: objective single-author narratives, opinion-based primary source quotations, and facts and statistics. The clearly written objective narratives provide context and reliable background information. Primary source quotes are carefully selected and cited, exposing the reader to differing points of view, and facts and statistics sections aid the reader in evaluating perspectives. Presenting these key types of information creates a richer, more balanced learning experience.

For better understanding and convenience, the series enhances information by organizing it into narrower topics and adding design features that make it easy for a reader to identify desired content. For example, in *Compact Research: Illegal Immigration*, a chapter covering the economic impact of illegal immigration has an objective narrative explaining the various ways the economy is impacted, a balanced section of numerous primary source quotes on the topic, followed by facts and full-color illustrations to encourage evaluation of contrasting perspectives.

The ancient Roman philosopher Lucius Annaeus Seneca wrote, "It is quality rather than quantity that matters." More than just a collection of content, the *Compact Research* series is simply committed to creating, finding, organizing, and presenting the most relevant and appropriate amount of information on a current topic in a user-friendly style that invites, intrigues, and fosters understanding.

Teens, Nutrition, and Dieting at a Glance

What Are Humans *Supposed* to Eat?

Humans evolved to eat a wide variety of foods. However, many scientists believe that humans are not designed to eat large quantities of processed foods.

Special Nutritional Needs

Because teens are growing, they have increased caloric needs. They also need certain vitamins and minerals as their brains and bodies grow and mature.

Teen Athletes' Needs

Some teen athletes need thousands more calories than active teens. They can also improve their athletic performance by eating the right foods before, during, and after intense exercise.

The Risks for Teen Athletes

Teens who compete in weight-dependent sports like wrestling or gymnastics are at increased risk of developing eating disorders.

The Rise in Teen Obesity

Since the 1980s, rates of teen obesity have increased from one in twenty to one in five.

Why Is Teen Obesity on the Rise?

No one is sure why today's teens are gaining weight. Popular theories are more fast-food consumption, more processed foods, and more sugar in the diet.

The Food Industry's Role

Because of food-processing technology, the industry can manipulate levels of salt, sugar, and fat to make people eat more.

The Dangers of Dieting

Unhealthy dieting can lead to fatigue, nutritional deficiencies, weight gain, and eating disorders in some teens.

How Can Teens Lose Weight Safely?

Teens have the best chance of losing weight and keeping it off by eating a healthy diet, avoiding sugar and processed foods, and increasing exercise.

Overview

❝Ask yourself, Would Grandma consider this food? Does it look like something that might occur in nature? It's pretty much common sense: you want to buy food, not unidentifiable food-like objects.❞

—Mark Bittman, chef and author who writes about food policy, health, and nutrition.

❝Nutrition science is very sketchy. It's very young science, and they change their mind a lot about what we need to eat. Digestion and food itself are still mysteries we're trying to unpack.❞

—Michael Pollan, author and director of the Knight Program in Science and Environmental Journalism at the University of California–Berkeley.

According to a 2012 food and health survey by the International Food Information Council Foundation, more than three-fourths of consumers find it hard to know what to believe about diet and nutrition information. In fact, the report found that "most Americans (52 percent) have concluded that figuring out their income taxes is easier than knowing what they should and shouldn't eat to be healthier."[1] Teenagers who want to lose weight, get in shape, or improve their health find diet and nutrition information especially confusing because most dietary advice is aimed at adults and does not take into consideration the special nutritional needs of growing adolescents.

What Are Humans *Supposed* to Eat?

Like pigs, chickens, and raccoons, human beings are omnivores, meaning that they eat both plants and animals. Because humans can eat a wide variety of foods, they can live—and thrive—in almost every environment on earth. For instance, in the past, people living in the Arctic lived long and healthy lives eating only the meat and fat of fish, birds, and marine mammals. Many members of the Masai tribe in Africa eat only cattle products and are well known for their tall stature and overall excellent health. On the other hand, people living on the Japanese island of Okinawa eat a diet made up almost completely of plants and are some of the longest-lived people in the world.

Over hundreds of thousands of years, humans evolved to be able to digest a wide range of plants and animals. However, almost none of the foods that humans evolved to eat are eaten today. About ten thousand years ago, the human diet changed significantly as people moved from hunter-gatherer to agriculturally based societies. This change caused humans to significantly increase their consumption of carbohydrates, and fossil records show that humans lost about 4 inches (10 cm) in average height as a result.

Since then, the food supply has been modified by selective breeding (allowing only plants and animals with specific traits to reproduce), by factory farming and food-processing practices, and most recently by genetic engineering. According to archaeological scientist Christina Warinner, almost every species of plant and animal humans eat today would be unrecognizable to people living ten thousand years ago. For instance, the bananas sold in grocery stores do not exist in the wild. "Every banana you've ever eaten is a genetic clone of every other banana, grown from cuttings," Warinner explains. "If you were to eat a wild banana, it is so full of seeds that . . . [many people] wouldn't even recognize it as edible."[2]

> **Because humans can eat a wide variety of foods, they can live—and thrive—in almost every environment on earth.**

Controversy Among Nutrition Scientists

Even though foods have changed, most are still healthy. But many processed and convenience foods are not, and these have been blamed for rises in rates of obesity, diabetes, heart disease, cancer, and other illnesses

Studies on the importance of eating breakfast are inconclusive in connection with weight loss and weight gain. Studies show that successful dieters tend to eat breakfast but not that eating breakfast had any effect on their efforts to lose weight.

and conditions. The role of nutritional science is to determine exactly what types and proportions of foods constitute a healthy diet and which are detrimental to our health.

Unfortunately, this scientific field is fraught with controversy. For instance, the dramatic increase in obesity among teenagers since the 1980s has been blamed on processed foods, excess sugar and carbohydrates, high-fat foods, and even growth hormones given to farm animals. In addition, genetics seem to play a big part in how each individual's body reacts to the foods he or she eats. Some people can eat anything they like and still remain at a normal weight, living a long, healthy life. Others must restrict certain foods or gain excess pounds or develop diet-related diseases.

One of the problems that nutritional scientists face is that it is difficult to conduct well-designed research studies about the interplay between diet, obesity, and health. "Most of our dietary recommendations are based on studies that try to measure what people eat and then follow them for years to see how their health fares," explains science journalist Nina Teicholz. "The data that emerge from these studies are weak and impressionistic."[3] People tend to make mistakes when they report what they eat, so results can be unreliable. In addition, studies that control what participants eat—such as those conducted in a hospital setting—are usually too expensive to go on for more than a few weeks. For this reason, scientists tend to conduct small studies that last only a few weeks. They also frequently analyze the results from other studies instead of generating new data. This can create a situation in which dozens of scientists publish findings that are based on a single research trial of a small number of people.

Also, the media tends to report a correlation (when two things occur at the same time but are not necessarily related) as causation (when one thing causes another). For instance, one common "fact" about nutrition is that skipping breakfast causes a person to overeat and gain weight. Although skipping breakfast does make it harder for teens to concentrate and learn in school, it has not been proved to cause weight gain. A 2013 report in the *American Journal of Clinical Nutrition* found that past research was based only on observational data that showed that successful dieters tend to eat breakfast. As *New York Times* science writer Anahad O'Connor explains, these observational studies "showed only that eating breakfast was a common behavior among people who were actively trying to avoid regaining weight, just as diet soda might be a common drink of choice among dieters but not necessarily the cause of their weight loss."[4]

> " It is difficult to conduct well-designed research studies about the interplay between diet, obesity, and health. "

Despite the uncertainty in nutritional science, there are still many things that all scientists agree on. Humans must eat adequate amounts of protein and fat to survive, either from plant or animal sources. Carbohydrates are not absolutely necessary for life, but they do provide the most efficient source of energy and, in their natural state, contain important vitamins and minerals. Finally, without essential nutrients, humans become malnourished, develop diseases, and can eventually die.

What Is a Nutrient?

A nutrient is a substance that is essential for growth and maintenance of life. There are two types of nutrients: micronutrients and macronutrients. The prefaces *micro* and *macro* mean "small" and "large," respectively, and refer to whether a small or a large amount of the nutrient must be ingested.

Macronutrients are eaten in large quantities and provide energy. There are three basic macronutrients: protein, carbohydrate, and fat. Most foods contain all three macronutrients, but usually one macronutrient is primary. For instance, a cup of potatoes has about ten times the amount of carbohydrate as protein. On the other hand, a handful of almonds has about the same amount of protein and carbohydrate.

Micronutrients are vitamins and minerals essential to good health. There are about thirty micronutrients necessary for normal growth and maintenance of human life. When food is left in its natural state, it is rich in these micronutrients. However, food processing and some cooking practices can strip away many naturally occurring vitamins and minerals. Sometimes these foods are then fortified or enriched by adding vitamins and minerals back into the food.

What Is a Calorie?

A calorie is a measure of energy. The calories associated with food are actually kilocalories, or kcals—though they are almost always referred to as calories. One kcal is the amount of heat energy needed to raise one kilogram of water one degree Celsius.

Calories are not good or bad—they are necessary to power our bodies. However, some calories are referred to as "empty." Foods that contain empty calories are not nutrient dense; they provide the body with energy but contain very few vitamins or minerals. Highly processed foods like candy, cake, and alcohol are made up of empty calories. Empty calorie foods are often easy to consume in excess because they usually contain very little fiber—indigestible plant material that slows digestion and the release of energy. Empty calories often cause a burst of energy followed

> Calories are not good or bad—they are necessary to power our bodies.

by lethargy and a craving for more empty calories. This can cause over-eating, weight gain, and disease.

Nutrient-dense, fiber-rich foods include whole fruits, vegetables, and whole grains. These foods provide steady, lasting energy that is released into the bloodstream over several hours.

What Is Protein?

Every cell in the human body contains protein. Dietary protein is nec-essary for all cell growth and repair, a process that is accelerated dur-ing childhood and adolescence. Protein is made up of twenty different amino acids. The body can make some of these, but nine of them are essential, meaning that they must be ingested in the diet. A food that contains all nine amino acids, such as meat or fish, is called a complete protein. A food that contains only some amino acids, like beans, is called an incomplete protein.

Good sources of animal protein are lean meats, fish, and low-fat dairy. For instance, an egg contains six grams of protein, a serving of low-fat Greek yogurt contains seventeen grams of protein, and a chicken breast contains thirty grams of protein. Plants also contain some protein, though they are usually incomplete proteins (exceptions are the whole grains buckwheat and quinoa). For instance, a cup of broccoli contains 2.6 grams of protein, a cup of rice contains 4.4 grams of protein, and two tablespoons of peanut butter contains 8 grams of protein.

What Is Fat?

Like protein, fat is essential for life. Both animals and plants store energy as fat, which makes fat in the diet an excellent source of concentrated energy. Fat on the body helps to carry out many chemical reactions, store essential vitamins, and insulate and protect vital organs.

There are two basic types of fat in foods: saturated and unsaturated. These terms refer to the chemical structure of the fat molecules and whether they are fully saturated with hydrogen atoms. Saturated fat (like butter, animal fat, and coconut oil) tends to stay solid at room tempera-ture, while unsaturated fat (like olive oil and fish oil) tends to be liquid at room temperature. Unsaturated fats are generally very healthy. Saturated fats are thought to contribute to cardiovascular disease, though some scientists now disagree with this theory. However, most doctors still en-

> "Saturated fats are thought to contribute to cardiovascular disease, though some scientists now disagree with this theory."

courage their patients to follow the recommendations of the US Department of Agriculture (USDA), which urges people to limit saturated fat to 10 percent of their diet.

Because many fats degrade and burn when heated or spoil over time, food scientists developed a very stable form of unsaturated fat called trans fat. Trans fat (also called partially hydrogenated oil) does not burn or become bitter when exposed to high heat, so it is often used in deep-frying. It also does not spoil—which is why many baked goods, such as crackers and snack cakes, can sit on the shelf for years and still taste good. Unfortunately, trans fats have been proved to contribute to cardiovascular disease and are now considered to be unhealthy.

What Are Carbohydrates?

Carbohydrates are found in plants such as fruits, vegetables, and grains. During digestion, carbohydrates are converted to a nonsweet form of sugar called glucose—which is the main source of energy in the modern diet. There are two basic types of carbohydrates: simple and complex. Simple carbohydrates are short molecules that are broken down into glucose quickly, providing immediate energy. Table sugar, candy, and fruit juices are all examples of simple carbohydrates.

Complex carbohydrates are carbohydrates that still contain fiber— the indigestible part of plants. (Fiber is also considered to be a carbohydrate, but since it cannot be digested, it has no calories.) Fiber causes the conversion to glucose to happen much more slowly, which results in a slow and steady release of energy. Whole fruits and vegetables and whole grains like wild rice and wheat berries are complex carbohydrates.

Although simple carbohydrates are often referred to as sugars and complex carbohydrates are often referred to as starches, refined flour products like white bread, pasta, and white rice are generally considered to be simple carbohydrates. Since all the fiber has been removed, these starches convert to glucose as quickly as sugars.

Health experts have long advised that teens who want to lose weight exercise and include plenty of fruits, vegetables, and whole grains in their diet. In recent years, advice for teen dieters has also included eating fewer refined carbohydrates.

How Important Is Good Nutrition for Teens?

Good nutrition is important for everyone, but it is especially important for teens because their bodies are still growing. Inadequate nutrition and making poor food choices can result in a host of health problems. For instance, a lack of protein in the diet can cause fatigue, poor skin, weak nails, a lowered immune system, and—in extreme cases—stunted growth and a delay in the onset of puberty. Too much saturated or trans fat in the diet can cause high levels of fat in teenagers' blood, which can lead to heart disease in later life. Excess simple carbohydrates in the diet has been linked with both obesity and type 2 diabetes—a disease that occurs when the body can no longer remove glucose (sugar) from the blood and that was once unheard of in teenagers. Finally, eating too many processed foods and too few whole fruits and vegetables can cause a variety of vitamin and mineral deficiencies.

How Can Teen Athletes Improve Performance Through Diet and Nutrition?

Compared with their nonathletic counterparts, teen athletes have special dietary and nutritional needs. They usually need extra calories to meet their increased energy requirements and extra protein to repair and build muscle. A diet made up of lean protein, healthy fats, and a variety of whole, unprocessed carbohydrates like fruits, vegetables, and whole grains will usually provide enough nutrients for the average teen athlete, though doctors still recommend supplementing with a daily multivitamin designed for teenagers.

> A lack of protein in the diet can cause fatigue, poor skin, weak nails, [and] a lowered immune system.

Depending on the sport, a teen athlete may also want to bulk up, slim down, or increase strength, speed, or endurance. Athletes can use a combination of diet and exercise to achieve these goals and to optimize their performance. However, teens should be wary of adopting unhealthy eating patterns in an attempt to change their bodies or their weight for their chosen sport. Athletes who consistently take in fewer calories than they need in an attempt to meet weight requirements risk developing eating disorders. "I'd say about 95 percent of the wrestlers (at Princeton) have had an eating disorder at one time,"[5] said a member of Princeton's wrestling team. Experts believe that most unhealthy eating patterns among athletes begin when the athlete is going through puberty—the time when adolescents need the most calories.

In addition, there is an entire industry of performance-enhancing pills, powders, foods, and drinks, all of which claim to improve athletic performance. Some of these products can be useful; for instance, vegetarian or vegan teen athletes can benefit from a daily high-quality protein shake, and teens who play lengthy matches or run long distances can successfully replenish their glucose stores with a sports drink. However, many performance products make claims that have not been proved or

> **Teens should be wary of adopting unhealthy eating patterns in an attempt to change their bodies or their weight for their chosen sport.**

even tested, and some contain herbs, supplements, and other substances not regulated by the Food and Drug Administration (FDA). Some also contain caffeine and other drugs that can be dangerous to teens—especially young teenagers and those of smaller stature.

Why Are More Teenagers Overweight Today?

Most overweight teens are extremely motivated to lose excess weight, yet obesity rates continue to rise. In the 1980s about one in twenty teenagers were obese. Today one in five teens suffer from obesity. Obesity rates have also increased in adults, small children, and even infants. Not only can being overweight or obese cause dangerous health problems in teens, it can also affect quality of life, making it harder to exercise, participate in sports, and enjoy outdoor activities. It can also have a negative social and emotional impact and lead to lower self-esteem.

Scientists know that something in the environment is causing weight gain, but they cannot agree on what that something is—or what to do about it. Some blame a decrease in exercise coupled with a prevalence of high-fat, high-calorie foods, whereas others blame an increase of sugar and refined carbohydrates. Most experts also put some of the blame on the food industry. Food science has become extremely sophisticated, and scientists can manipulate tastes and textures with salt, sugar, fat, and other substances to make foods almost irresistible. Some doctors even argue that sugar is mildly addictive, creating cravings and withdrawal symptoms similar to drugs like cocaine. One thing is clear—until the cause of teenaged obesity is determined, it will be difficult to reverse.

What Constitutes Healthy Weight Loss?

Most health and nutrition groups—including the Centers for Disease Control and Prevention (CDC) and the Obama administration's Let's Move campaign—claim that the best way for teens to lose weight is to eat less and move more. They prescribe increased exercise and a low-calorie, low-fat diet that includes fruits, vegetables, and whole grains. This advice has not changed much since the 1980s, when the government first began recommending cutting fat from the diet. However, rising obesity rates indicate that this may not be the best approach to weight loss. An increasing number of scientists are proposing another solution: to limit carbohydrates, especially sugar and other highly refined carbs, and to allow more protein and fat in the diet. Since both fat and protein reduce appetite, most people following lower-carbohydrate diets naturally eat fewer calories.

> **Until the cause of teenaged obesity is determined, it will be difficult to reverse.**

Although it is still not clear which approach works best for weight loss, recent studies indicate that low-carbohydrate diets may be slightly more effective than low-fat diets—for at least some people. "Over the last ten years there have been research studies all over the world that say a low carbohydrate diet is a healthy thing to do," explains Dr. Eric Westman, director of the Duke Lifestyle Medicine Clinic at Duke University. "In fact, it is therapeutic for obesity, diabetes, high blood pressure, heartburn, fatty liver—the list goes on and on."[6] However, teens who follow this approach may be in danger of not getting enough essential nutrients, and experts warn that they should not attempt low-carbohydrate dieting without checking with their doctor.

It is also becoming clear that restrictive weight-loss diets that are designed to be followed for a short period of time are far less successful than making dietary changes that can be sustained for a lifetime. Low-fat diets that leave the dieter hungry, low-carb diets that severely restrict food choices, and various fasting and fad diets all may cause initial weight loss, but as soon as the diet is over the weight is regained. This can herald a cycle of yo-yo dieting that can slow down the metabolism and cause weight to increase over time. It can also lead to an obsession with food and thinness that can manifest as an eating disorder.

Do the Research—and Talk to a Doctor

Teenagers who want to improve their health through diet and nutrition may receive a great deal of conflicting advice, especially if they want to lose weight. The more they understand about the science of nutrition—what happens to various foods after they are eaten—the easier it will be to make sound nutritional choices.

How Important Is Nutrition for Teens?

66The phenomenal growth that occurs in adolescence, second only to that in the first year of life, creates increased demands for energy and nutrients.99

> —Mary Story, nutritional scientist and director of the Healthy Eating Research program at the University of Minnesota.

66Eating patterns established in childhood often track into later life.99

> —USDA and US Department of Health and Human Services, government organizations that publish the official dietary guidelines for Americans.

Adolescence—the years between childhood and adulthood—is a time of rapid growth and development. At the onset of puberty, which often begins in the preteen years, individuals experience an intense physical growth spurt that lasts two to four years. Adolescents do not just get taller; their bodies gain muscle, bone, and fat mass. According to the Centre for Adolescent Health in Melbourne, Australia, "During the growth spurt in puberty, teenagers do enough growing to achieve approximately 15% of their total adult height and 40% of their total adult weight!"[7]

To power this growth spurt, adolescents need more calories than humans do at any other time of life, which is why their appetite often increases. This hunger is normal; it is nature's way of making sure teens eat enough to fuel healthy development.

What Does a Growing Body Need?

According to the American Academy of Pediatrics, boys need about 2,800 calories per day, and girls need about 2,200 calories per day. As teens move into later adolescence, their calorie needs decrease somewhat, but not always. "Kids who are big and tall or who participate in physical activity will still need increased amounts of energy into late adolescence,"[8] says nutritional scientist Mary Story.

The type of calories teens eat is also extremely important. Teens need the right proportion of protein, fat, and carbohydrates, as well as adequate vitamins and minerals, to assure healthy growth and development. Experts recommend that teenage girls consume at least forty-six grams of protein a day and teenage boys at least fifty-two grams. Larger, more muscular, or more active individuals need more protein. It is not unusual for teenaged athletes to eat eighty grams of protein daily. In addition, at least 30 percent of daily calories should come from fat, saturated fat should be limited to 10 percent of total daily calories, and trans fat should be avoided. Most experts also recommend that teenagers get 50 to 60 percent of their daily calories from complex carbohydrates like whole fruits, vegetables, and whole grains.

> " Adolescents need more calories than humans do at any other time of life. "

Teens who eat the correct proportion of protein, fat, and carbohydrates can still develop nutritional deficiencies if those calories do not contain adequate vitamins and minerals. According to experts at Oregon State University, because "adolescents are increasingly consuming energy-rich, nutrient poor diets comprised of fast food, processed foods, and sugar-sweetened beverages . . . many adolescents do not come close to meeting intake recommendations for nutrient-rich foods."[9] This puts teenagers at risk for vitamin and mineral deficiencies, which in turn can affect development and even delay puberty. For this reason, teens should avoid poor quality or "empty" calories, such as sugar and white flour products. In addition, most doctors recommend that all teenagers take a multivitamin designed for adolescents to assure they get the minimum daily requirements of most vitamins and minerals.

Do Girls and Boys Have Different Nutritional Needs?

In general, girls and boys need the same amounts of vitamins and minerals. However, girls usually need fewer calories than boys. For instance, during later adolescence, girls eat roughly 25 percent fewer calories per day than do boys. Because girls eat less, they have an increased risk of developing vitamin and mineral deficiencies.

> **Because girls eat less, they have an increased risk of developing vitamin and mineral deficiencies.**

Calcium and vitamin D deficiencies are especially common in teen girls. Vitamin D helps the body absorb calcium, and both of these nutrients are crucial for healthy bone development. Studies have shown that teen girls who take vitamin D supplements absorb more calcium and develop stronger bones, which may reduce the incidence of osteoporosis later in life.

Teenaged girls who are menstruating are also particularly susceptible to anemia, or iron deficiency. According to Health.com, "Iron deficiency is the most common nutritional deficiency in the United States, and women are among those at greatest risk."[10] Iron helps make hemoglobin, a protein that helps red blood cells deliver oxygen throughout the body. A lack of iron can cause increasing fatigue and worsen heart problems. Dietary iron is found in animal protein, beans, and green leafy vegetables. Teenaged girls should be especially careful to get enough iron in their diets.

Which Plate?

Many experts recommend that teenagers follow the guidelines published in the USDA's *Dietary Guidelines for Americans*, which were last published in 2010 and are expected to be revised in the fall of 2015. The USDA separates certain daily servings of five food groups: protein, fruits, vegetables, grains, and dairy. Recommendations are designed to supply teens with adequate nutrients to sustain them through adolescence. The USDA represents these foods' recommended serving sizes in a graphic called My-Plate, which has replaced the traditional food pyramid. The plate shows the proportions of different foods that should make up an average meal.

Many scientists disagree with the USDA's nutritional recommendations, however, and especially with the foods that the USDA chooses to include in each of its food groups. The Harvard School of Public Health has developed the Healthy Eating Plate as an alternative to MyPlate, which it argues has been shaped by "intense lobbying efforts by a variety of food industries."[11] The Healthy Eating Plate eliminates dairy as a food group, removes potatoes and beans from the vegetable group, adds a healthy oils group, and recommends restricting fruit juice.

Dairy and the Role of Calcium

Calcium is an essential mineral found in dairy products (such as yogurt, milk, and cheese), fish with edible bones (such as sardines and some brands of canned salmon), and many vegetables (such as turnip greens and kale). Many foods are also fortified with the mineral, such as orange juice and soy milk.

Calcium is crucial for bone growth and maintenance, especially among teens. The National Institutes of Health recommends that adolescents aged nine to eighteen eat thirteen hundred milligrams of calcium each day—about three hundred milligrams above adult recommendations. According to the National Institutes of Health, "Bones increase in size and mass during periods of growth in childhood and adolescence, reaching peak bone mass around age 30. The greater the peak bone mass, the longer one can delay serious bone loss with increasing age. Everyone should therefore consume adequate amounts of calcium and vitamin D throughout childhood, adolescence, and early adulthood."[12] Bone loss due to calcium deficiency can eventually lead to osteoporosis, a disease of later life in which bones become so weak and brittle that they fracture very easily.

> "Calcium is crucial for bone growth and maintenance, especially among teens."

Because calcium is so important, the USDA considers dairy to be a food group and recommends that dairy products such as milk, cheese, or yogurt be eaten at every meal. However, the Harvard School of Public Health does not include dairy in its Healthy Eating Plate. Its website states that "there is little if any evidence that high dairy intakes protect against osteoporosis, and there is considerable evidence that too-high intakes can be harmful. . . . High intakes are associated with increased risk of prostate cancer and possibly ovarian cancer."[13] Harvard recommends that dairy be limited to one or two servings a day and additional calcium be obtained from other healthy sources.

A common reason for a calcium deficiency is a lack of vitamin D in the diet. The skin makes vitamin D when exposed to sunshine; it is also found in fatty fish like salmon and tuna. The use of sunscreen blocks the skin's ability to make vitamin D and can lead to a calcium deficiency. However, since sunscreen is an excellent way to protect against skin cancer, most experts recommend that teens eat foods that contain vitamin D, eat vitamin D fortified foods, or ask their doctor if a supplement is necessary.

Making Sense of Fats

Scientists' understanding of how different types of fat affect health is still evolving. According to science educator George Zaidan, most scientists currently believe that "it's not how much fat you eat, it's what kind of fat."[14] Unsaturated fat—such as the fat in olive oil, nuts and seeds, and fatty fish like salmon—is considered to be very healthy. Many of these fats contain healthy omega-3 fatty acids that protect against disease. They also raise levels of large cholesterol molecules (high-density lipoprotein, or HDL) in the bloodstream, which protects the heart. (HDL is sometimes referred to as "good cholesterol.")

Saturated fat, such as the fat found in meat and dairy products, is thought to be unhealthy in excess because it can raise levels of small cholesterol molecules (low-density lipoprotein, or LDL), which can increase the risk of heart disease and stroke. (LDL is sometimes referred to as "bad cholesterol.") However, some scientists are reexamining this hypothesis. These scientists think that a moderate amount of high-quality saturated fat in the diet may be harmless because it also raises HDL, canceling out the damaging effects of LDL. However, until this controversy is settled, most experts advise that saturated fat be kept to less than 10 percent of total calories.

One thing that scientists agree on is the danger of trans fat. Trans fat has been proved to be harmful to health because it raises LDL significantly without raising HDL. Experts recommend that people check the list of ingredients for the words "partially hydrogenated" to identify hidden trans fat.

The USDA does not include fat as a food group. At one time it recommended that total fat be kept under 30 percent of total calories. However, it now recommends limiting only saturated fat because of the heart-protective effects of healthy oils. In this area, the Harvard School of Public Health agrees. "The percentage of calories from fat that you eat, whether high or low, isn't really linked with disease," it notes on its website. "The key to a healthy diet is to choose foods that have more good fats than bad fats—vegetable oils instead of butter, salmon instead of steak—and that don't contain any trans fat."[15]

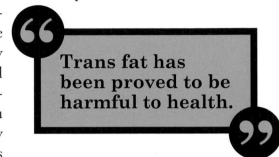

Trans fat has been proved to be harmful to health.

Eating a Vegetarian Diet

Many teens choose to eat a vegetarian or vegan diet for ethical reasons or to improve their health. Generally, vegetarians do not eat meat, but there are many types of vegetarians—some eat eggs and dairy, and some also eat fish and seafood. A very strict form of vegetarianism is called veganism. Vegans do not eat any animal products, including eggs, dairy, or even honey.

Vegetarians—especially vegans—often risk developing a protein deficiency and can also be deficient in iron and B vitamins, which are found in meat. To get adequate protein, vegetarians often eat soy products (like tofu) and combine plant foods into complete proteins (like beans and rice). Vegetarians who are athletes or who have a lot of muscle mass need more protein. For this reason, some experts suggest adding a quality protein shake to the diet to supplement protein.

Some vegetarians are extremely healthy. But vegetarians who eat a lot of sugar, refined grains, and other simple carbohydrates run the same health risks as nonvegetarians of developing diet-related conditions like obesity and diabetes. One food that can be problematic for vegetarians is the white potato. The USDA has placed potatoes in the vegetable group, and many vegetarians consider potatoes to be a healthy source of calories. However, some experts warn that white potatoes are essentially simple carbohydrates because they are converted immediately to glucose (sugar) in the body. According to the Harvard School of Public Health, "A cup of potatoes has a similar effect on blood sugar as a can of Coca Cola or a handful of jelly beans." It warns that "over the long term, diets high in potatoes and similarly rapidly-digested, high carbohydrate foods [such as white rice and pasta] can contribute to obesity, diabetes, and heart disease."[16]

Teens who choose vegetarian diets should avoid processed foods and simple carbohydrates and favor whole, intact foods. Good choices for vegetarians include brown rice and beans, intact grains like quinoa and wheat berries, nuts and seeds, and whole fruits and vegetables.

The Consequences of Poor Nutrition

Poor nutrition can stunt growth, delay puberty, and cause disease. However, in the United States nutritional deficiencies rarely reach these levels. Early signs of poor nutrition include a lack of energy, skin problems, lackluster hair, and brittle nails. A lack of protein in the diet can cause fatigue, hair loss, and a lowered immune system. Too much saturated or trans fat can cause high fat levels in the blood, and not enough healthy fat can also prevent the absorption of some nutrients from vegetables. In addition, an excess of simple carbohydrates has been linked with metabolic syndrome, which can lead to diabetes in teens.

Teens who do not get adequate nutrition often do not perform well in school or extracurricular activities. According to the National Health and Nutrition Examination Survey, children with poor nutrition are more likely to miss school due to illness. Poor nutrition has also been linked to depression, anxiety, attention-deficit/hyperactivity disorder, and learning disabilities.

Challenges to Eating a Healthy Diet

Nutrition is never so important as during the adolescent years, when teens are growing and maturing. However, this time of life can be especially difficult for teens to make good food choices. Teens are often reliant on others to provide healthy meals. Plus, teens tend to be on the go and rely heavily on convenience foods, which are often low in nutrients. For all of these reasons, teens must be especially vigilant about their diets. Learning to prepare healthy meals and snacks at home can be a good first step to eating a more healthful diet.

Primary Source Quotes*

How Important Is Nutrition for Teens?

> 66 Carbohydrate is not a required or essential nutrient. People don't have to eat carbohydrate because your body can make all the carbohydrate it needs internally. 99

—Eric Westman, "The Science Behind Low Carb High Fat," lecture presented at the Central Coast Nutrition Conference, San Luis Obispo, California, June 24, 2014.

Westman is a professor of medicine and the director of the Duke Lifestyle Medicine Clinic at Duke University.

> 66 Carbohydrate comes from plant-based foods. Saying we don't need carbohydrate is to say we don't need plant-based foods. And I dispute that. 99

—T. Colin Campbell, "Atkins vs. the China Study Diet," debate hosted by UAB Center for Palliative and Supportive Care, April 16, 2013. http://vimeo.com/64139406.

Campbell is a professor of nutritional biochemistry at Cornell University.

Bracketed quotes indicate conflicting positions.

* Editor's Note: While the definition of a primary source can be narrowly or broadly defined, for the purposes of Compact Research, a primary source consists of: 1) results of original research presented by an organization or researcher; 2) eyewitness accounts of events, personal experience, or work experience; 3) first-person editorials offering pundits' opinions; 4) government officials presenting political plans and/or policies; 5) representatives of organizations presenting testimony or policy.

Primary Source Quotes

66 Eat food, not too much, mostly plants. 99

—Michael Pollan, interviewed by Josh Zepps on HuffPost Live, May 13, 2014. http://live.huffingtonpost.com.

Pollan is an author and the director of the Knight Program in Science and Environmental Journalism at the University of California–Berkeley.

66 Red meat is one of the healthiest foods you can eat. 99

—Chris Kresser, "Red Meat: It Does a Body Good!," *Chris Kresser* (blog), 2015. http://chriskresser.com.

Kresser is a functional medicine practitioner who writes about alternative health and nutrition.

66 Teen vegetarians can be unhealthy eaters too, so don't be fooled that 'vegetarian' necessarily equals slim and healthy. 99

—Jill Castle, "Got a Teen Vegetarian? Here's What You Need to Know," *Just the Right Byte* (blog), December 4, 2014. http://jillcastle.com.

Castle is a registered pediatric dietitian and nutritionist.

66 Three meals per day are three opportunities to get in good nutrition. 99

—Sarah Muntel, "Kid's Corner: Teens & Tweens—Why Nutrition Is Important," Obesity Action Coalition, 2015. www.obesityaction.org.

Muntel is a registered dietitian and the bariatric coordinator with Community Health Network in Indianapolis.

❝The biggest hoax in the world is taking grains, processing them to death, and then adding fiber back in and claiming they're high fiber.❞

—Mark Bittman, interviewed by Josh Zepps on HuffPost Live, May 7, 2014. http://live.huffingtonpost.com.

Bittman is a chef and author who writes about food policy, health, and nutrition.

❝The need for an absolute total fat requirement is not necessary—it's the quality of the fat.❞

—Miriam Nelson, comments at the 2015 Dietary Guidelines Advisory Meeting, September 16, 2014.

Nelson is director of the John Hancock Research Center on Physical Activity, Nutrition, and Obesity Prevention.

How Important Is Nutrition for Teens?

- The USDA estimates that teens eat less than **half** of the fruit, vegetables, and fiber recommended by its dietary guidelines.

- A 2009 study published in *Nutrition Research Reviews* found that eating a healthy breakfast is associated with improved memory, reduced absenteeism in school, and improved mood.

- The President's Council on Fitness, Sports, and Nutrition estimates that **16.7 million** children experience food insecurity (limited availability of safe and nutritional foods).

- According to the Vegan Resource Group, about **4 percent** of children and teens are vegetarian or vegan.

- According to the US Department of Health and Human Services, **3 of the top 10** leading causes of death in the United States are strongly associated with poor nutrition (heart disease, stroke, and diabetes).

- According to pediatric endocrinologist Robert Lustig, **80 percent** of the food in the modern grocery store contains added sugar.

- According to the CDC, empty calories such as those from soda, fruit drinks, dairy desserts, grain desserts, and pizza make up **40 percent** of daily total calories for children aged **2 to 18**.

Two Plates

In response to what it considered to be deficiencies in the USDA's visual nutrition guide MyPlate, the Harvard University School of Public Health developed an alternate nutrition guide called the Healthy Eating Plate. Differences include recommending a greater proportion of vegetables, including healthy oils, and eliminating dairy as a separate food group.

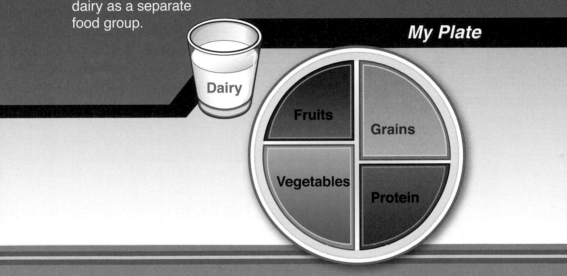

My Plate

Dairy

Fruits

Grains

Vegetables

Protein

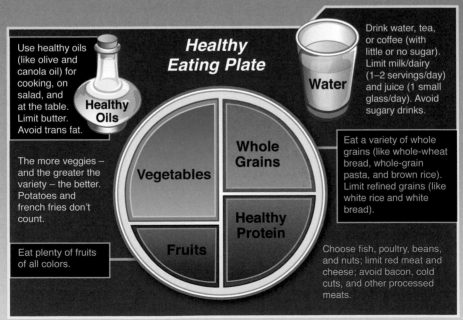

Healthy Eating Plate

Use healthy oils (like olive and canola oil) for cooking, on salad, and at the table. Limit butter. Avoid trans fat.

Healthy Oils

The more veggies – and the greater the variety – the better. Potatoes and french fries don't count.

Eat plenty of fruits of all colors.

Water

Drink water, tea, or coffee (with little or no sugar). Limit milk/dairy (1–2 servings/day) and juice (1 small glass/day). Avoid sugary drinks.

Vegetables

Whole Grains

Healthy Protein

Fruits

Eat a variety of whole grains (like whole-wheat bread, whole-grain pasta, and brown rice). Limit refined grains (like white rice and white bread).

Choose fish, poultry, beans, and nuts; limit red meat and cheese; avoid bacon, cold cuts, and other processed meats.

Sources: US Department of Agriculture, www.choosemyplate.gov; Harvard School of Public Health, "Healthy Eating Plate & Healthy Eating Pyramid," www.hsph.harvard.edu.

Daily Nutritional Guidelines for Girls and Boys

The USDA's *2010 Dietary Guidelines for Americans* recommends total daily calorie intakes for young people based on age and gender. To ensure that children get adequate nutrients, it also recommends how many servings of each of the five food groups should be consumed each day. Calories and servings are estimations; teens who are active or who have more muscle mass will need to eat more.

	Girls		Boys	
	Aged 9–13	**Aged 14–18**	**Aged 9–13**	**Aged 14–18**
Calories (depends on growth and activity level)	1,400–2,200	1,800–2,400	1,600–2,600	2,000–3,200
Protein (ounces)	4–6	5–6.5	5–6.5	5.5–7
Fruits (cups)	1.5–2	1.5–2	1.5–2	2–2.5
Vegetables (cups)	1.5–3	2.5–3	2–3.5	2.5–4
Grains (ounces)	5–7	6–8	5–9	6–10
Dairy (cups)	2.5–3	3	3	3

Source: Mayo Clinic Staff, The Mayo Clinic, "Nutrition for Kids: Guidelines for a Healthy Diet," July 9, 2014. www.mayoclinic.org.

- The 2012 national Youth Risk Behavior Survey found that among high school students, **7 percent** did not eat vegetables, **5 percent** did not eat fruit or drink fruit juice, and **14 percent** did not eat breakfast in the 7 days before the survey.

- A 2015 study by the Illinois Prevention Research Center found that **1 in 5** children eat pizza on any given day. On days when teens eat pizza, they consume an additional **230 calories**.

Smart Snacks Sold in School

The Healthy, Hunger-Free Kids Act of 2010 requires that all foods sold in schools meet nutrition standards set by the USDA. These standards set limits on calories, salt, sugar, and fat, and promote snack foods that have whole grains, low fat dairy, fruits, vegetables, or protein as their main ingredients. Many states and individual schools have even stronger nutritional standards.

Shows empty calories*

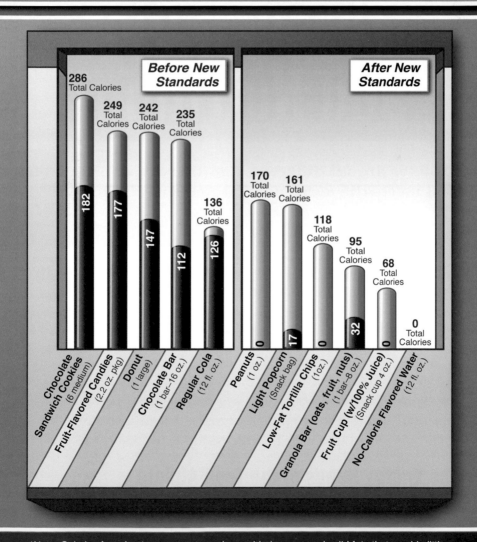

Before New Standards

286 Total Calories — Chocolate Sandwich Cookies (6 medium) — 182
249 Total Calories — Fruit-Flavored Candies (2.2 oz. pkg) — 177
242 Total Calories — Donut (1 large) — 147
235 Total Calories — Chocolate Bar (1 bar–16 oz.) — 112
136 Total Calories — Regular Cola (12 fl. oz.) — 126

After New Standards

170 Total Calories — Peanuts (1 oz.) — 0
161 Total Calories — Light Popcorn (Snack bag) — 17
118 Total Calories — Low-Fat Tortilla Chips (1oz.) — 0
95 Total Calories — Granola Bar (oats, fruit, nuts) (1 bar–8 oz.) — 32
68 Total Calories — Fruit Cup (w/100% Juice) (Snack cup 4 oz.) — 0
0 Total Calories — No-Calorie Flavored Water (12 fl. oz.)

*Note: Calories from food components such as added sugars and solid fats that provide little or no nutritional value. Empty calories are part of total calories.

Source: Centers for Disease Control and Prevention, "Competitive Foods in Schools," October 16, 2014. www.cdc.gov.

How Can Teen Athletes Improve Performance Through Diet and Nutrition?

❝Athletes are all different, and there is no single diet that meets the needs of all athletes at all times.❞

—Ron Maughan, professor of sport and exercise nutrition at Loughborough University in the United Kingdom, and Louise Burke, professor of sports nutrition at Australian Catholic University in Melbourne, Australia, and the team dietitian for the Australian Olympic team from 1996 to 2012.

❝There is a strong emphasis on weight and appearance for high school . . . athletes in today's culture.❞

—Sports Nutrition, a free online training course offered by the National Federation of State High School Associations that trains athletes, parents, and coaches on how teen athletes can achieve optimal nutrition.

When it comes to eating right, student athletes face many challenges. According to dietitian Molly Kimball, teens who play sports must balance "the demands of classes, study time, after-school (and sometimes before-school) practice, as well as friends and family, all the while trying to maximize their energy, performance, and recovery."[17]

The Energy Needs of the Teen Athlete

Teen athletes are not only growing; they expend more energy than the average active teen. They also tend to have more muscle mass—which requires extra calories to sustain. For these reasons, athletic teens need to ingest more calories. According to the American Academy of Family Physicians, "Teen athletes . . . may need as many as 5,000 calories daily"[18]—which is thousands more calories than even an active teen needs. Calorie requirements vary and depend on body mass, activity level, and individual metabolism.

Most sports nutritionists recommend that teen athletes eat small meals and snacks throughout the day instead of eating only at mealtimes. Eating frequent small meals not only keeps energy levels constant, it improves performance. Digestion takes energy, which is why people often feel sluggish after a large meal and attempting to exercise after eating a large meal can cause nausea. As Dr. Luis E. Palacio, director of sports medicine at Northern Nevada Medical Center, explains, "Frequent eating ensures that the athlete's high-energy needs are met, while decreasing the gastrointestinal discomfort associated with consuming large meals."[19] Good snacks are those that contain complex carbohydrates, such as whole grain bagels, fresh fruit, and granola bars.

> " Eating frequent small meals not only keeps energy levels constant, it improves performance. "

The Importance of Carbohydrates

Carbohydrates are the most efficient and rapidly available source of energy for the teen athlete. For this reason experts recommend that most of an athlete's calories come from carbohydrates, which, according to the National Federation of State High School Associations, could be anywhere from three hundred to six hundred grams of carbohydrates each day.

Carbohydrates are important for athletes because they can be quickly converted into glycogen, a form of glucose stored in the muscles. Athletes rely on glycogen for both strength and stamina. Most people have more than enough glycogen stored in their muscles to sustain them through a typical sixty-minute workout. However, teen athletes often practice or play sports for many hours a day, which can deplete their glycogen stores. For this reason, it is important to refuel before, after, and sometimes even during exercise sessions.

How to Refuel with Carbohydrates

When refueling the body with carbohydrate-rich foods, it is important to consider how long the food will take to digest. Foods that contain fiber (complex carbohydrates), protein, or fat remain in the stomach longer and therefore take longer to convert to glycogen. In general, meals that digest more slowly, such as pasta dishes or sandwiches, should be consumed three or four hours before exercise. Lighter foods, including simple carbohydrates such as fruit juice or crackers, can be eaten one to two hours before exercise or during exercise sessions that last more than one hour.

Athletes can actually benefit from eating rapidly digested simple carbohydrates right before or during exercise because they are immediately burned for fuel. According to diet and fitness expert Diane Lynn, "Complex carbohydrates give longer lasting energy, but simple carbohydrates give high school endurance athletes a boost during long events or practices."[20] Teen athletes may have to experiment to find foods that provide immediate energy but do not cause stomach upset or interfere with performance. Examples include fruit, watered-down juice, or sports drinks.

It is also important that athletes eat a light snack and rehydrate within thirty minutes to two hours after physical activity so that they can start replenishing their glycogen stores. Muscles are most able to store glycogen immediately after a workout, so it is important for athletes to take advantage of this time—especially those who have trouble eating enough to meet their energy needs. "Students who fail to refuel and rehydrate sufficiently after sports and other physical activities will not have the optimal level of hydration and energy to practice or compete as safely at the same intensity and level of performance the next day," says Dr. Mick Koester, former chair of the National Federation of State High School Associations Sports Medicine Advisory Committee. "Nutrient deficiencies from low food intake can lead to increased risk for early fatigue, stress fractures and other injuries."[21] He recommends that athletes bring carbohydrate-rich snacks to eat after away games that have long travel times.

Sports Drinks and Energy Foods

Even though many sports drinks contain vitamins, minerals, and various other supplements, they are primarily made up of water, sugar, and salt. Athletes who simply need to rehydrate should avoid sports drinks—especially those that contain caffeine, which can worsen dehydration. However, sports drinks can be useful to restore energy during exercise that lasts longer than an hour or to replenish glycogen after that exercise. "A less expensive alternative is to dilute any fruit juice by about half with water,"[22] advise nutritional experts at Brown University.

The problem with sports drinks is that they are often consumed by nonathletes or by athletes when they are not exercising. According to Tim Noakes, director of the Research Unit for Exercise Science and Sports Medicine at the University of Cape Town in South Africa, "Sugary sports drinks are promoted as essential for athletic performance, but are used predominantly by those without real athletic aspirations. Users need to understand that exercise may not protect them from the negative consequences of an excessive sugar intake."[23] If more sugar is consumed than the body can store as glycogen, it is turned into fat, which can lead to impaired athletic performance and diet-related disorders.

> " The problem with sports drinks is that they are often consumed by non-athletes or by athletes when they are not exercising. "

Processed sports performance foods such as energy bars or powdered shakes are also high in sugar. According to Meredith Melnick, editorial director of the *Huffington Post* Healthy Living column, "Some of the most popular bars . . . have more than 20 grams of sugar each, which is often the same as a packet of candy."[24] Energy bars should be treated like sports drinks and only used as a source of quick-acting carbohydrates during or directly after intense exercise. Despite this, teenagers consume both far too frequently. In fact, the National Health and Nutrition Examination Survey found that soda and energy or sports drinks are third on the list of the top sources of daily calories for teens.

Energy Drinks Can Be Dangerous

Energy drinks are a type of beverage that increases alertness by adding high levels of stimulants—usually caffeine. Teens sometimes confuse energy drinks with sports drinks, but they are very different. Sports drinks are designed to be hydrating and to replace salt lost during sweating. But the caffeine and sodium in energy drinks are actually dehydrating and can impede performance.

According to dietitian Densie Webb, many energy drinks also include high levels of the amino acid taurine, which "is known to influence various physiological functions, including blood pressure, growth hormone production, and hypothalamus stimulation."[25] The effects of high taurine levels on adolescents is unknown. Energy drinks also include other ingredients that are touted to improve energy and performance. However, according to a study of the effects of energy drinks on athletes, "None of the other ingredients present in energy drinks and in the amounts in a can of energy drink actually produces a significant effect on physical or cognitive performance."[26] Most experts believe that these ingredients are added in small amounts for marketing purposes.

> "Teen athletes need the same micronutrients as nonactive teens. There is no evidence that increased amounts of vitamins or minerals enhance performance."

Energy drinks can be extremely dangerous for teens. Various studies, including a 2011 study published in the *Journal of Pediatrics*, has found that consuming energy drinks may increase the risk of strokes, heart palpitations, seizures, and sudden death in children and teens—especially in those who have underlying health problems like diabetes or hyperactivity disorders. According to the online health resource New Health Guide, "The scariest part about these studies is that the median age of those people affected is seventeen years old."[27]

Protein and the Teen Athlete

The body uses protein to repair muscle tissue and increase muscle mass after strength-building exercises. Teen athletes need extra protein—especially those who play sports that rely on strength. However, some athletes believe that the more protein they eat, the more muscle they will build. Experts at Brown University point out that this is not true. "Added protein intake alone will not build muscle. To see an increase in muscle mass, you will need to do strength training and add extra calories to your diet. These calories should be mostly in the form of extra carbohydrates, with only small amounts of additional protein."[28] The average diet of most student athletes contains adequate protein, and protein supplementation usually is not necessary.

Vitamins, Minerals, and Other Supplements

Teen athletes need the same micronutrients as nonactive teens. There is no evidence that increased amounts of vitamins or minerals enhance performance. Even electrolytes like salt and potassium that are lost through sweating can be easily replaced by eating a normal diet, which is plentiful in these minerals. Increasing levels of some micronutrients can even be harmful, especially the fat-soluble vitamins A, D, E, and K. Fat-soluble vitamins are stored in the fat cells and can build up in the body to dangerous levels. However, because most modern diets are deficient in micronutrients, most experts still recommend that all adolescents take a daily multivitamin.

Many supplements are advertised as being performance enhancing and are marketed to athletes. However, there has been no reputable evidence that any supplement increases performance without endangering health. Substances like ephedrine and natural steroids such as androstenedione can be extremely dangerous, especially to young people.

In addition, supplements are not regulated by the FDA and may contain less or more active ingredients than are listed on the label, additional ingredients, or contaminants. According to Brown University, "It is . . . practically impossible for you to know, as a consumer, whether what you purchase as a supplement is safe, will do what it says it does, or even contains in the bottle what it claims to have."[29] Many supplements are also banned by sports organizations like the National Collegiate Athletic Association, including some popular energy and vitamin drinks. Most experts warn against teenagers taking any supplements not prescribed by their doctor or sports nutritionist.

Making Weight

In sports that classify athletes by weight class (such as wrestling or boxing), it has become common practice for athletes to try to lose weight before a match so that they can compete in a lower weight class and gain an advantage. "Although I know it's good to keep hydrated, to make weight I sometimes completely cut liquids out of my diet," explains Josh, a teen who competes for a high school wrestling team. "[But] before a match or after weigh-ins I usually stuff my face with sports drinks, water, and food to gain my weight back so I can feel good before I wrestle."[30]

According to dietitian Bonnie Taub-Dix, the starvation-to-binge pattern is very common among wrestlers and can lead to an unhealthy relationship with food. As Josh admitted to her, "Wrestling has definitely affected my life in a way where I regularly don't eat normally. I constantly think about my weight and how much I weigh."[31]

Today sports nutritionists agree that quick weight-loss methods like fasting or deliberately dehydrating the body sap energy and impede performance; such methods can also lead to nutritional deficiencies and, in some people, eating disorders. Nutritionists suggest that athletes who want to "make weight" embark on a healthy and gradual weight-reduction program under the supervision of a medical professional. However, if teens are currently at a healthy weight, experts warn that attempting to reduce their weight can lead to chronic fatigue and underperformance and suggest that teens concentrate on maximizing their performance in their weight class by building muscle.

> " Quick weight-loss methods like fasting or deliberately dehydrating the body sap energy and impede performance. "

When Being Thin Matters in Athletics

In sports such as gymnastics, figure skating, and long-distance running, it is preferable to have a thin, lean body type. Athletes who compete in these sports must often severely restrict their caloric intake to remain at a competitive weight or body shape. This can become particularly difficult when a young athlete reaches puberty. According to the authors of a study on minimizing the health risks to these athletes, "The body of a young growing athlete often develops in a direction against the paradigm of the athlete's sport, especially in women and where the sport demands being as lean as possible."[32]

These young female athletes sometimes attempt to maintain their prepubescent body shape through extreme dieting, which can lead to what researchers call the Female Athlete Triad: cessation of menstruation (or delay of puberty), disordered eating, and calcium deficiency (which leads to osteoporosis). The Female Athlete Triad has not been studied extensively; however, studies of extreme dieting have shown it can lead to chronic fatigue, anemia (iron deficiency), eating disorders, and an increased risk of infection, illness, and injury. In addition, studies of young female gymnasts have found that extreme dieting during puberty can result in less bone mass and reduced height.

> **Studies of young female gymnasts have found that extreme dieting during puberty can result in less bone mass and reduced height.**

Athletes competing in weight-sensitive sports who do not consume enough calories often suffer from poor performance—the opposite of their intended result. Experts suggest that teens who struggle to maintain a low body weight to stay competitive discuss their difficulties with a health care professional who is familiar with the Female Athlete Triad.

Prioritize Good Nutrition

Many teen athletes believe that they must push their bodies and endure a certain level of pain and discomfort to succeed in their chosen sport. Experts warn that these teens should not extend that thinking to their diet. Teen athletes should not endure hunger or feel they must buy expensive performance foods; rather, they should meet their nutritional needs by eating a wide variety of whole foods.

Primary Source Quotes*

How Can Teen Athletes Improve Performance Through Diet and Nutrition?

66 Carbs are the only fuel that can be used for power moves—a slam dunk, a sprint to the goal line, or an overhead smash all need muscle carbohydrate. 99

—Christine Rosenbloom, "Teen Nutrition for Fall Sports," *Eat Right*, Academy of Nutrition and Dietetics, February 13, 2014. www.eatright.org.

Rosenbloom is a registered dietitian nutritionist and former chair of the positions committee of the Academy of Nutrition and Dietetics.

66 We endorse a low carbohydrate lifestyle for athletes ... [because] once you make this transition, you can then train harder, perform longer, and recover faster. 99

—Jeff Volek and Stephen Phinney, *The Art and Science of Low Carbohydrate Performance*. Beyond Obesity, 2012, p. 2. Kindle edition.

Volek is a professor of kinesiology at the University of Connecticut, and Phinney is a nutritional research scientist.

Bracketed quotes indicate conflicting positions.

* Editor's Note: While the definition of a primary source can be narrowly or broadly defined, for the purposes of Compact Research, a primary source consists of: 1) results of original research presented by an organization or researcher; 2) eyewitness accounts of events, personal experience, or work experience; 3) first-person editorials offering pundits' opinions; 4) government officials presenting political plans and/or policies; 5) representatives of organizations presenting testimony or policy.

❝ Frequent fueling is the name of the game when it comes to effectively optimizing athletic performance. ❞

—Molly Kimball, "Sports Nutrition: Fueling the Student Athlete," *New Orleans Times-Picayune*, September 16, 2014. www.nola.com.

Kimball is a registered dietitian who advises athletes on enhancing performance with nutrition.

....

❝ Athletes must know that if they have poor eating habits they will not achieve a higher level of athletic performance by simply using dietary supplements. ❞

—Mick Koester, Sports Nutrition (training course), National Federation of State High School Associations Learning Center, 2014. https://nfhslearn.com.

Koester is the former chair of the National Federation of State High School Associations Sports Medicine Advisory Committee.

....

❝ Young wrestlers need to learn that the number on the scale is not necessarily a reflection of their strength or state of health. ❞

—Bonnie Taub-Dix, "Wrestling with Their Weight . . . Literally," *U.S. News & World Report*, September 28, 2012. http://health.usnews.com.

Taub-Dix is an award-winning certified dietitian-nutritionist.

....

❝ Dehydration is the worst method of losing weight [for wrestlers] since it causes quick decline in strength, endurance and mental alertness. ❞

—Sports Medicine team at Children's Hospital Colorado, "Wrestlers: Tips on Losing Weight Safely—Avoiding Risky Weight Loss Behaviors," Children's Hospital Colorado Orthopedics Institute, 2014. http://orthopedics.childrenscolorado.org.

The Sports Medicine team at Children's Hospital Colorado educates athletes, parents, and coaches about nutrition and injury prevention.

....

66 The average . . . adolescent does not engage in enough physical activity to warrant consumption of sports drinks. **99**

—Mary Story and Laura Klein, "Consumption of Sports Drinks by Children and Adolescents," Robert Wood Johnson Foundation, June 2012. http://healthyeatingresearch.org.

Story is the director and Klein a senior researcher at the Healthy Eating Research program at the University of Minnesota.

66 Irregular cycles, stalled progress in the gym, and stagnant weight loss despite enormous efforts are [the female athlete's] body's cry for help and rest. **99**

—Vanessa Bennington, "What Really Causes Irregular Menstrual Cycles in Female Athletes?," Breaking Muscle, November 4, 2013. http://breakingmuscle.com.

Bennington is a nurse practitioner and a nutritional and physical trainer.

Facts and Illustrations

How Can Teen Athletes Improve Performance Through Diet and Nutrition?

- According to the National Federation of State High School Associations, an independent testing laboratory tested 58 sports performance supplements and found that **25 percent** of them contained unlisted anabolic agents (steroids or steroid-like substances) or stimulants.

- A 2011 study published in the *Journal of Sports Sciences* found that up to **94 percent** of elite athletes competing in weight-sensitive sports use dieting and extreme weight-control measures before competition.

- A 2012 study published in *Medicine & Science in Sports & Exercise* found that **28 percent** of elite athletes who suffered from eating disorders still had not recovered from them **15 to 20 years** after they stopped competing.

- Children's Hospital Colorado reports that **25 to 67 percent** of teenaged wrestlers use techniques like overexercise, fasting, and dehydration to lose weight.

- In 2013 the *British Journal of Sports Medicine* reported that only **48 percent** of physicians and **43 percent** of physiotherapists know how to identify female athletes who suffer from 1 or more of the components of Female Athlete Triad.

Dangers of Extreme Weight-Loss Behaviors

A 2013 study published in the *British Journal of Sports Medicine* reported that athletes who use extreme methods to control their weight may suffer serious health problems. In addition, these methods often adversely affect athletic performance.

Weight Control Behavior	Physiological Effects and Health Consequences	Effect on Performance
Fasting or starvation	Energy and nutrient deficiency, glycogen depletion, loss of lean body mass, a decrease in metabolic rate and reduced bone mineral density	Poor exercise performance due to general weakness, reduced ability to cope with pressure, depressed muscle force, and increased susceptibility for disease and injuries
Diet pills	Typically function by suppressing appetite and may cause a slight increase in metabolic rate. May induce rapid heart rate, anxiety, nervousness, inability to sleep, and dehydration. Any weight loss is quickly regained once use is discontinued.	Indirectly results in poor performance and may be classified as doping
Laxatives or enemas	Weight loss is primarily water and any weight lost is regained once use is discontinued. Dehydration and electrolyte imbalances, constipation, cathartic colon and steatorrhoea (excessive fat in the feces) are common.	May affect concentration and hydration status. May be addictive and athlete can develop resistance, thus requiring larger and larger doses to produce the same effect
Diuretics	Weight loss is primarily water and any weight lost is quickly regained once use is discontinued. Dehydration and electrolyte imbalances are not uncommon.	Poor performance and classified as doping
Self-induced vomiting	Large losses of water in the body can lead to dehydration and electrolyte imbalances. Gastro-intestinal problems, including pesophagitis, esophageal perforation, and esophageal ulcers may occur.	May lead to electrolyte imbalances. Largely ineffective in promoting weight (body fat) loss
Saunas	Dehydration and electrolyte imbalances can occur in extreme cases.	Weight loss is primarily water and any weight is quickly regained once fluids are replaced.
Excessive exercise	If combined with low energy availability it will increase risk of staleness, chronic fatigue, illness, overuse, injury, and menstrual dysfunction.	Experience the effect of lack of recovery

Source: *British Journal of Sports Medicine*, Jorunn Sundgot-Borgen, et al., "How to Minimize the Health Risks to Athletes Who Compete in Weight-Sensitive Sports," November 2013, p.1,014.

Eating Plan for Game Day

Teen athletes can maximize their performance by eating the right foods at the right times. They should eat large amounts of complex carbohydrates four to five hours before an event, and small amounts of simple carbs just before it. Teens should also eat carbs within four hours after a game or heavy practice session, lest they deplete their energy stores for the next day.

Timing	Meal/Snack	Examples
4–5 hours before event (may need snack later to prevent hunger)	**Heavy meal:** Generous amount of carbohydrate (50–60 g) Moderate protein Moderate fat	Baked chicken, potatoes, fruit, bread, and fluids or Peanut butter sandwich, baked chips, fruit, and fluids
2–4 hours before event	**Light Meal:** Moderate amount of carbohydrate (30–40 g) Small amount of fat Moderate protein	Turkey sandwich, pretzels, fruit, and fluids
1/2 –1 hour before event	**Snack:** Small amount of carbohydrate (15–30 g) Limited amount of fat	Pretzels and fluids (e.g., sports drink or water)
Within 4 hours after event	**Sports drink or snack:** Generous amount of carbohydrate	Gatorade, lemonade, fruit, fig bar, or crackers

Source: American Dietetic Association, "Sports Nutrition for Teen Athletes," www.fusdweb.com.

- According to the National Federation of State High School Associations, if teen athletes do not eat and drink after intense exercise sessions, it can take up to **36 hours** for their energy reserves to be replenished.

- According to food and nutrition expert Sukhsatej Batra, most female teen gymnasts need between **2,000 and 2,400 calories** per day.

In Some Male Sports, Disordered Eating Prevalent

Eating disorders have long been thought to mainly affect females. However, a recent study found that many male athletes who compete in weight-dependent sports develop disordered eating (abnormal eating behaviors, such as habitual dieting) to lose weight or maintain lower weights. A 2013 Brazilian study of 156 male athletes found that over one-fourth reported disordered eating behaviors. Disordered eating has been know to lead to disorders like anorexia and bulimia.

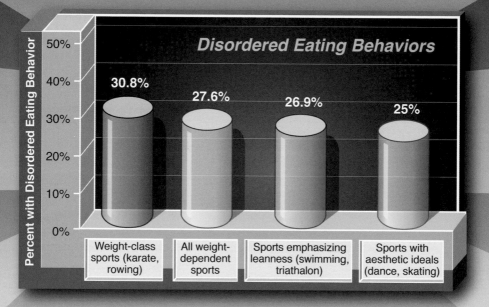

Source: Eating Disorder Review, "What Increases the Risk of Eating Disorders in Male Athletes?," 2014. http://eatingdisordersreview.com.

- In 2010, **4 football players** in Orange County, California, were taken to the emergency room with rapid heart rates after drinking caffeinated energy drinks.

- According to sports nutrition experts at Brown University, consuming protein powders or supplements does not increase muscle mass.

- According to a 2011 study by Yale University, **27 percent** of parents think that sports drinks are healthy for children.

The Female Athlete Triad

The Female Athlete Triad describes three distinct but interrelated conditions that can occur in female athletes: disordered eating (habitual dieting or undereating), menstrual dysfunction (missed periods or delay in onset of menstruation), and osteoporosis (low bone mass). These conditions result from overexercising, not eating enough nutrients, or both. The Triad is most often seen in teens who play sports that emphasize low body weight, either for aesthetic or performance purposes, such as gymnastics, cheerleading, running, rowing, and ice skating.

Disordered Eating
- Anorexia
- Bulimia

Menstrual dysfunction
- Delayed menarche
- Absence of menstrual cycle

Osteoporosis
- Increased risk of stress fractures
- Low bone density

Source: Regional Sports Medicine, "The Female Athlete Triad," December 4, 2013. http://regionalsportsmedicine.org.

- A 2014 study published in the *Journal of Nutrition Education and Behavior* found that sports and energy drink consumption among teens was related to higher video game use, sugary beverage intake, and smoking.

- A 2008 study published in the *Journal of Bone and Mineral Research* found that female navy recruits taking part in basic training who also took calcium and vitamin D supplements had **20 percent** fewer stress fractures than female recruits who did not take supplements.

Why Are More Teens Overweight Today?

66Kids are obese for two reasons. They have voracious appetites, and they don't exercise enough. It's that simple.99

—Steven Arnold King, US representative for Iowa's fourth congressional district.

66Childhood obesity is a disease of the environment. It's a natural consequence of normal kids with normal genes being raised in unhealthy, abnormal environments.99

—Dr. Yoni Freedholf, assistant professor of medicine at the University of Ottawa.

More teens are overweight and obese today than ever before. In the 1980s one in twenty adolescents were obese; today one in five are. Various studies have shown that teens are heavier now than at any other time in history. The question that scientists have not yet been able to answer is why.

The Difference Between Overweight and Obese

Scientists use a measurement called body mass index, or BMI, to determine if a person's weight is in the normal range for his or her height. BMI is expressed as a ratio of a height and weight. In the United States a BMI of 18.5 to 25 is considered normal, 25 to 30 is considered overweight, and 30 and above is considered obese.

BMI can be an inaccurate measure of overall health, especially if a person is muscular (for instance, many top athletes have BMIs in the obese range). But for most teens, a BMI in the overweight or obese range is unhealthy. The CDC estimates that more than two-thirds of adults and one-third of teens are either overweight or obese. Estimates by various governmental agencies place the number of obese teenagers at 17 to 21 percent—or about one in five teens.

The Dangers of Excess Weight

Excess weight can have serious consequences for teenagers—especially if that weight is stored in the abdomen, which causes a person to have an apple shape or a potbelly. This abdominal fat (also called visceral fat) is a sign of a dangerous condition called metabolic syndrome. Most health organizations define metabolic syndrome as having three out of five conditions: obesity, high blood sugar, high levels of fat in the blood (cholesterol and triglycerides), high blood pressure, and cardiovascular disease.

Metabolic syndrome can lead to type 2 diabetes, fatty liver disease, heart attack and stroke, many cancers, and even dementia and Alzheimer's disease. Although it was once rare for teenagers to have these weight-related illnesses, they are on the rise among teens. According to *USA Today*, the latest data available shows that the prevalence of type 2 diabetes among teens increased by 30 percent from 2000 to 2009, and the *New York Times* reports that in the past two decades, incidence of fatty liver disease in teens has more than doubled.

> **Excess weight can have serious consequences for teenagers.**

Being overweight or obese does not just affect physical health. According to psychologist Rebecca Puhl, obese teens often experience weight bias. Weight bias can manifest as bullying and social exclusion by peers, reduced expectations from teachers, and even teasing by parents. "Consequences of weight bias can substantially reduce a child's quality of life,"[33] Puhl writes. Teens who are victimized because of their weight are vulnerable to depression, anxiety, and low self-esteem. They are also three times more likely to contemplate or attempt suicide than over-weight teens who are not victimized.

What Is Causing Teens to Be Overweight or Obese?

All scientists agree that something has changed in the environment since the 1970s that is causing a dramatic rise in obesity among teenagers. Some experts believe that fiber-rich, plant-based foods have been replaced in the teen diet with cheap, highly palatable convenience foods, and these are causing teens to overeat. Others say that teens spend too much time sitting—either watching TV or on their computers or hand-held devices. And a growing number of experts believe that high levels of refined carbohydrates and sugar in the teen diet—especially those found in sweetened beverages—are causing teenagers to gain weight.

To date, no one can say for certain why teenagers are struggling with obesity in greater and greater numbers. The truth is probably a combina-tion of factors. "There isn't any one thing that causes obesity," says Jessica Rieder, associate clinical professor of pediatrics at Children's Hospital at Montefiore/Albert Einstein College of Medicine. "It's not just genetics, society, environment, or family. It's all of them."[34]

Energy Imbalance and Weight Gain

Weight gain is caused by an energy imbalance in the body. When a per-son takes in more calories than his or her body needs, the excess is stored as fat. Almost all experts agree that teens are heavier today because they are eating more calories than their bodies are burning. According to esti-mates by the USDA, all Americans, including teens, eat about 300 more calories per day on average than they did in the 1970s. Teens are also less aerobi-cally fit, which is the result of not getting enough exercise. The CDC reported that only 52.4 percent of children aged twelve to fifteen had adequate levels of fitness in 2000. By 2012 that number dropped to 42.2 percent.

Some people believe that increases in teen obesity have finally peaked. Data collected from the National Health and

> " Teens are heavier today because they are eating more calories than their bod-ies are burning. "

Nutrition Examination Survey (NHANES) reveals that calorie consumption among teens remained steady from 1999 to 2010; on average, boys ate about the same number of calories and girls ate slightly fewer calories. In response, overall obesity rates among teens began to level off during that time period, reaching about 18.4 percent in 2010. "To reverse the current prevalence of obesity, [decreases in] these numbers have to be a lot bigger," said Marion Nestle, a professor of nutrition at New York University. "But they are trending in the right direction, and that's good news."[35] However, NHANES data from 2011 to 2012 indicated that the percentage of obese teens increased again, reaching 20.4 percent. This suggests that teen obesity rates may still be trending upward.

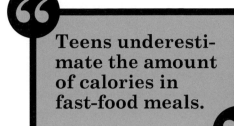

> Teens underestimate the amount of calories in fast-food meals.

Teens Who Eat Out Eat More

Though the increase in calorie consumption explains the rise in obesity among teens, it does not explain why teens are eating more than they were in the 1970s. One theory is that the way teens eat has changed. Since the 1970s teens have been getting more of their calories from fast-food restaurants—from 6.5 percent in 1977 to 1978 to 17 percent in 2003 to 2006 (the most recent data available). Studies have also shown that teens are eating out more frequently. A 2013 study published in *JAMA Pediatrics* reports that frequent fast-food consumption (three or more times a week) among adolescents has increased in recent years from 19 percent to 27 percent for females and 24 percent to 30 percent for males. Some experts believe that one reason for the increase may be that restaurants are becoming a common social destination for teens, replacing shopping malls.

The problem is that teens seem to have trouble estimating how much they are eating when they eat out. A 2013 study published in the medical journal *BMJ* found that American teens underestimate the amount of calories in fast-food meals by as much as 34 percent. According to one of the study's authors, Dr. Jason Block, "Teens . . . are consuming more calories than they think they're getting when they eat fast food"[36]—about 260 calories more, the study found. Multiple studies also confirm that when teens overeat processed food, they do not compensate by eating fewer calories during the rest of the day. Obesity researchers Lisa M. Powell and Binh T. Nguyen believe that this may be why teens are eating more over-all. "Upward trends in fast-food consumption have paralleled increasing obesity rates among children and adolescents,"[37] Powell and Nguyen state.

The Role of the Food Industry

Fast food is not the only type of food implicated in the obesity epidemic. Since the 1930s technological advances in food processing have made most of the food teens eat cheaper and tastier but less healthful. Processed foods, which are high in calories and low in nutrients, now flood the food supply, and many believe they are the cause of the obesity epidemic.

Foods are deliberately manipulated by the food industry so that people will overeat them.

Dr. David Kessler, former commissioner of the FDA, explains that these foods are deliberately manipulated by the food industry so that people will overeat them. In his book for teens, *Your Food Is Fooling You*, he writes, "Food companies make [processed] foods with very large amounts of three ingredients—sugar, fat, and salt. . . . These kinds of foods make us fat because they make us want to eat more."[38]

Kessler explains that each of these ingredients makes the experience of eating more pleasurable. Fat makes food feel thicker in the mouth and taste richer, salt enhances flavor, and sugar releases opioids and dopamine in the brain in much the same way that cocaine does, causing people to feel good and driving them to want more. Restaurant food is often layered with these three ingredients to create a strong sensory response. One example Kessler gives is cheese fries. "The potato base is a simple carbohydrate. That quickly breaks down to sugar in the body. Once it's fried and layered with cheese, we're eating salt on fat on fat on sugar,"[39] he explains.

Food Marketing Targets Young People

Kessler also explains that the food industry deliberately targets young people in its marketing. "Fast food restaurants, high-energy drinks, candy bars, and other snacks are all heavily advertised to teens,"[40] he states. According to data collected by the consumer information company Nielsen, in 2012 preschoolers viewed 2.8 fast-food ads on TV every day, children aged six to eleven viewed 3.2 ads, and teens viewed 4.8 ads. These advertisements are usually full of triggering images that associate food with feelings of fun and well-being.

> **When fiber is removed from sugar, it can have a devastating effect on metabolism.**

Kessler believes that the food industry targets young children because early consumption of highly palatable, sugar-laced foods seems to interfere with their natural ability to regulate their calorie intake later in life. He notes a study at the University of Colorado that found that drinking a sugary beverage caused kids to overeat the rest of the day: Five-year-olds ate 20 percent more, eight-year-olds ate 40 percent more, and eleven-year-olds ate 70 percent more. "In other words," Kessler explains, "as kids got older, they were losing their ability to stop eating when they felt full."[41] Kessler believes that by the time children become teenagers, these overeating patterns have become well established, resulting in chronic overeating and teenage obesity.

Is Sugar Fattening?

Some experts believe that this rise in overeating among teens is driven by one ingredient that the food industry has added to almost all of its highly palatable processed foods: sugar. Robert Lustig, a pediatric endocrinologist who treats obese children and teenagers, believes that high levels of sugar in the teen diet is actually changing their bodies' biochemistry and driving them to overeat.

Sugar is a carbohydrate made up of two molecules: glucose and fructose. Fructose is what gives sugar its sweetness, and in nature it is always bound up with fiber. (In fact, except for honey, fructose never exists in nature without fiber.) Lustig believes that when fiber is removed from sugar, it can have a devastating effect on metabolism.

In a complex metabolic process described in his book *Fat Chance: Beating the Odds Against Sugar, Processed Food, Obesity, and Disease*, Lustig explains that when eaten in large quantities over time, sugar raises levels of the fat-storing hormone insulin. Insulin then blocks the appetite-suppressing hormone leptin, which normally tells the brain that there is enough fat in storage. "If your brain thinks there's no leptin, you're pretty miserable," Lustig explains. Without the leptin signal, the brain thinks the body is starving and it "goes into conservation mode, driving down your energy expenditure, physical activity, and quality of life . . . [and] driving up your appetite."[42] In other words, excess sugar in the diet makes teens feel tired and hungry, causing them to move less, eat more, and gain weight.

Lustig believes that increased sugar in the diet is driving the obesity epidemic among teens. He states that sugar accounts for four-fifths of the overall increase in carbohydrate consumption since the 1980s. Twenty to 25 percent of calories consumed now come from sugar, and some teenagers consume 40 percent of their calories from sugar. In addition, 33 percent of sugar consumption comes from beverages such as sodas, sports drinks, and juice. Lustig tells his young patients that it is crucial to stop drinking sweetened beverages. "There is not one biochemical reaction in your body, not one, that requires dietary fructose," he states. "Dietary sugar is completely irrelevant to life."[43]

Is There a Solution?

To date, there is no agreement about what is causing teens to eat more, move less, and gain weight. Without knowing this, it is very difficult to formulate a solution to the overall problem. However, understanding how different kinds of foods have contributed to the obesity epidemic can help teenagers identify their own issues with food and overeating. Teens should look at which foods they tend to eat to excess: high-fat foods, refined starchy carbohydrates, sweet foods, or processed foods engineered to be highly palatable. Avoiding foods that trigger overeating and replacing them with whole foods in their natural state may help prevent further weight gain and may even promote weight loss.

Primary Source Quotes*

Why Are More Teens Overweight Today?

66 Getting the junk food out of our schools is the obvious next step in our efforts to address the childhood obesity crisis. 99

—Mission: Readiness, *Still Too Fat to Fight*, 2012, p. 6. www.rwjf.org.

Mission: Readiness is an organization of more than five hundred retired senior military officers that works to help children overcome barriers such as obesity that would prevent them from serving in the military as adults.

66 Banning 'junk food' has become the trendy way to tackle [obesity in schools]. . . . Physical education offers more promise. 99

—Center for Consumer Freedom, "Physical Education Linked with Lower Childhood Obesity," June 18, 2013. www.consumerfreedom.com.

The Center for Consumer Freedom is a nonprofit lobbying organization that represents the fast-food, meat, alcohol, and tobacco industries.

Bracketed quotes indicate conflicting positions.

* Editor's Note: While the definition of a primary source can be narrowly or broadly defined, for the purposes of Compact Research, a primary source consists of: 1) results of original research presented by an organization or researcher; 2) eyewitness accounts of events, personal experience, or work experience; 3) first-person editorials offering pundits' opinions; 4) government officials presenting political plans and/or policies; 5) representatives of organizations presenting testimony or policy.

❝Overweight children and teens who are bullied are often called names, punched, teased, ganged up on, humiliated and ignored relentlessly.❞

—JoAnn Stevelos, "Bullying, Bullycide and Childhood Obesity," Obesity Action Coalition, 2015. www.obesityaction.org.

Stevelos is the former director of the Center for Best Practices for the Prevention of Early Childhood Obesity.

❝Obese fifth graders were more likely to remain obese in tenth grade if they perceived themselves to be much heavier than ideal.❞

—American Academy of Pediatrics, "Study Examines Patterns of Obesity Between Childhood and Adolescence," November 10, 2014. www.aap.org.

The American Academy of Pediatrics is a professional association of pediatric health care providers.

❝I'm football material, but my legs will go out on me sometimes. I want my diabetes to go away so I can do what everyone else can do.❞

—Davion, interviewed in *Bite Size*, directed by Corbin Billings. Los Angeles: Bond/360 Films, 2014. www.bitesizemovie.com.

Davion is a twelve-year-old middle school student who suffers from obesity.

❝One chocolate bar, that's your whole day's calories—but it's affordable within a [young teen's] pocket money. It's about educating them to make the right choices.❞

—Mary Sparrow, interviewed by Emma Birchley in "Child Obesity 'Leveling Off' but Concerns Remain," Sky News, January 30, 2015. http://news.sky.com.

Sparrow is the principal of City Academy Norwich in the United Kingdom.

66 Many obese adolescents were obese children. . . . They've already had a decade of obesity.99

—Ponrat Pakpreo, interviewed in *Our Supersized Kids*. Spokane, WA: KSPS Documentaries, 2013. http://video.ksps.org.

Pakpreo is a pediatrician who specializes in adolescent medicine.

66 Parents often feel that kids will outgrow being overweight, and I always tell them—not likely to happen.99

—Keith Ayoob, interviewed in ABC News, "Experts Saying Parents Are Underestimating the Weight of Their Children," August 1, 2014. http://abcnews.go.com.

Ayoob is a pediatric nutritionist and an associate professor at Albert Einstein College of Medicine.

66 Obese children have a quality of life comparable to children with cancer.99

—Rebecca Puhl, "Child Obesity and Stigma," Obesity Action Coalition, 2015. www.obesityaction.org.

Puhl is a clinical psychologist and the coordinator for Community and Weight Stigma Initiatives at Yale University.

Facts and Illustrations

Why Are More Teens Overweight Today?

- According to the National Institutes of Health, more than **one-third** of children are overweight or obese.

- According to the CDC, in the 1980s only **5 percent** of adolescents were obese. Today **20 percent** are obese.

- A study published in the *American Journal of Clinical Nutrition* found that from 2000 to 2010, the age group that showed the greatest rate of increase in obesity was **two- to five-year-olds**.

- According to the documentary *The Weight of the Nation*, children aged **2 to 17** see **12 to 21 commercials** for foods high in fat, sugar, or salt each day. Watching these commercials is thought to be a contributing factor in obesity.

- According to former FDA commissioner David Kessler, the average young person enters adulthood **18 pounds heavier** today than 4 decades ago.

- The Robert Wood Johnson Foundation reports that **20.2 percent** of African American and **22.4 percent** of Latino children aged **2 to 19** were obese in 2011 to 2012, as compared to **14.3 percent** of Caucasian children.

- According to the CDC, among obese **five- to seventeen-year-olds, 70 percent** had at least 1 risk factor for cardiovascular disease.

Rates of Severe Obesity Increasing Among Young People

A 2014 study published in *JAMA Pediatrics* found that while increase in the rates of overall obesity among children and teens has leveled off, the rates of severe obesity has increased. The study analyzed rates of obesity in youth aged two to nineteen years old and found that rates of class 3 obesity (a BMI of more than 40) had increased the most. The authors note that discussing overall rates of obesity can mask the increases in severe obesity among young people, which carries the greatest health risks.

Growth in Childhood Obesity Rates

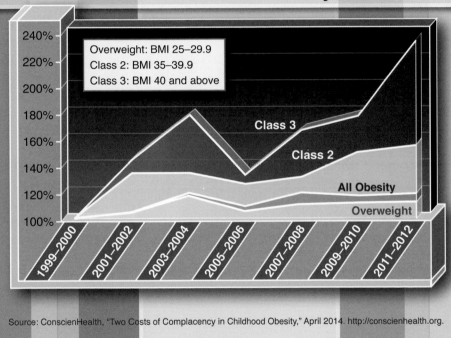

Source: ConscienHealth, "Two Costs of Complacency in Childhood Obesity," April 2014. http://conscienhealth.org.

- Diabetes, which is caused by metabolic dysfunction and linked to obesity, is the seventh leading cause of death in the United States.

- A 2012 study in the journal *Pediatrics* estimates that nearly **1 in 4** American teens may be on the verge of developing type 2 diabetes or could already be diabetic.

Teens Eat the Most Sugar

A 2008–2012 study of eating habits in the United Kingdom found that teens ate more sugar than any other age group. Teens ate over 74 grams of added sugar each day, the equivalent of 18.5 teaspoons. 15.6 percent of their daily calories came from added sugars. The World Health Organization advises that people get 5 percent of their daily calories from sugar.

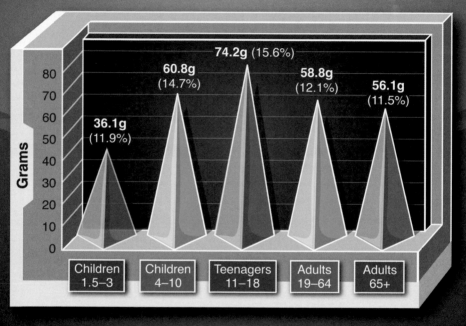

Source: Christine Jeavans, "How Much Sugar Do We Eat?," BBC News Health, June 26, 2014. http://www.bbc.com.

- The National Collaborative on Childhood Obesity Research reports that obese teenagers have an **80 percent** chance of becoming obese adults.

- The Robert Wood Johnson Foundation estimates that childhood obesity is responsible for **$14.1 billion** in direct health care costs each year in the United States.

- According to pediatric endocrinologist Robert Lustig, some teenagers consume **40 percent** of their calories from sugar.

What Constitutes Healthy Weight Loss?

❝I started with the Atkins Diet and other programs but it wasn't anything I felt like I could do forever. . . . I realized that I needed a lifestyle change.❞

—Daniel, a teen who successfully lost weight at MindStream Academy, a weight-loss center for teens who suffer from severe obesity.

❝There is simply no reason to be pushing children into weight reduction diets. . . . Dieting is a gateway drug to eating disorders.❞

—Laura Collins Lyster-Mensh, eating disorder activist and executive director of Families Empowered and Supporting Treatment of Eating Disorders.

Weight fluctuations are a normal part of physical development for teenagers. When adolescents hit puberty, their appetites increase and they begin to accumulate fat to power growth spurts. However, when weight gain gets out of control, teens often turn to dieting as a solution to losing weight.

Which Diet Is Most Effective for Weight Loss?

Most reputable diets fall into two groups: low-fat, calorie-restricted diets; and high-fat, carbohydrate-restricted diets. Calorie-restriction diets reduce calorie intake with low-fat foods and portion control. Carbohydrate-reduction diets reduce sugar and carbs by replacing grains and starchy vegetables with fat or by promoting unprocessed foods. Nonreputable diets, or "fad" diets, usually work by drastically reducing calories. Fad diets are usually unsustainable, either because they cause extreme fatigue, extreme hunger, or both.

In general, the results of various types of reputable diets all seem to be about the same. A recent yearlong study of 148 men and women funded by the National Institutes of Health found that people on low-carbohydrate diets tend to lose about 8 pounds (3.6 kg) more a year than those on low-fat diets. They also had greater fat loss and improved risk factors for cardiovascular disease. However, the study's results were not definitive. "To my knowledge, this is one of the first long-term trials . . . [of a diet] without calorie restrictions,"[44] said Dariush Mozaffarian, dean of the Friedman School of Nutrition Science and Policy at Tufts University. Many more studies must be done before experts can claim that one diet is more effective than another.

> "Losing weight by severely cutting calories is not sustainable."

One thing that experts do agree on is that losing weight by severely cutting calories is not sustainable for most people and not advisable for teenagers, who need enough nutrients for healthy growth and development. Permanent changes in eating habits that cause slow and steady weight loss is the best—and healthiest—way to lose weight and keep it off. "You need to find a weight-loss approach that you can embrace for life,"[45] advise experts at the Mayo Clinic.

Low-Fat, Calorie-Restricted Diets

Calorie-restricted diets are based on the principal of energy balance. Weight is lost when more calories are burned than are consumed. These diets tend to limit calories by limiting fats. Fat has 9 calories per gram, whereas protein and carbohydrates have 4 calories per gram. Most doctor-recommended calorie-restricted diets limit total fats to no more than thirty grams per day. Diets that restrict fat further can leave the dieter hungry and unsatisfied. One reason for this is that the fat content in food increases satiety—the sensation of fullness that one gets after eating.

The most popular calorie-restricted diet is Weight Watchers. Weight

Watchers helps dieters eat a balanced, calorie-restricted diet by assigning foods point values. The system is easy to follow and assures that dieters get adequate nutrients while reducing calories enough to lose weight at a slow and steady rate.

One benefit of Weight Watchers is its support system. Members either attend weekly meetings or join an online community. Some drawbacks of the plan are price (members pay a weekly or monthly fee) and the time involved in tracking food. Dieters must keep track of points and weigh and measure their portions to accurately track their food consumption.

Other popular calorie-restricted diets are Jenny Craig and Nutrisystem. Both of these diet plans supply prepackaged meals to the dieter. Many people find this an effective way to lose weight because no measuring or calorie counting is necessary. However, these plans are expensive and are made up mostly of processed foods.

High-Fat, Carbohydrate-Restricted Diets

Carbohydrate-restricted diets are based on the concept that carbohydrates raise insulin levels, which promote fat storage and increase appetite. When fat takes the place of carbs in the diet, insulin levels go down and appetite decreases—resulting in lower calorie intake. Even though low-carb diets do not restrict calories, most experts say that people lose weight on them because they naturally eat less. "It's not that calories don't matter," explains Dr. Eric Westman. "People have a reduction in hunger, they eat less than they did before, and they start losing weight."[46]

> **People lose weight on [low-carb diets] because they naturally eat less.**

The most popular low-carbohydrate diet is the Atkins diet, developed in the 1970s by Dr. Robert Atkins. The Atkins diet restricts carbohydrates to as little as twenty grams per day and adds them back to the diet over time. Starchy foods, fruits, and some vegetables are eliminated from the early stages of the diet. Some people report that the diet causes intense cravings for carbohydrates and sugar—at least for the first few weeks. Others adapt well to the diet and are able to follow it long term.

Other low-carbohydrate diets include the South Beach Diet, Sugar

Busters, and the Paleo Diet. All of these diets limit carbohydrates to some extent. The Paleo Diet restricts foods to only those that were eaten in the Paleolithic period, before the advent of agriculture. Refined sugar, dairy, legumes, grains, and all processed foods are eliminated. Eighteen-year-old Joshua Weissman, who hosts the Paleo blog *Slim Palate*, lost more than 100 pounds (45 kg) when he stopped eating these foods and began following a Paleo-style diet. "I think the answer is for kids to eat nutrient-dense foods—something like a plate of organic grass-fed/pastured meat and fresh vegetables," he states. "Make fruit a treat, eat more vegetables and properly raised meat that's free of hormones and antibiotics, and enjoy plenty of healthy fats. See if that doesn't just change everything."[47]

Critics of low-carb diets claim that they include too many unhealthy fats, are too low in fiber, and exclude crucial nutrients. For these reasons, it is not recommended that teenagers go on a low-carb diet unless they get approval from their doctor.

The Mediterranean Diet

The diet most often cited by doctors as being both healthy and effective is the Mediterranean diet. According to *U.S. News & World Report*, "It's generally accepted that the folks in the countries bordering the Mediterranean Sea live longer and suffer less than most Americans from cancer and cardiovascular ailments."[48] This diet emphasizes fruits and vegetables; whole grains; beans, nuts, and legumes; fish and seafood; and healthy fats like olive oil. It limits sugar, refined grains like pasta and bread, and red meat. There is no single source for the Mediterranean diet, but the Harvard School of Public Health has developed a food pyramid to support it.

" Fad diets are really modified fasts. "

The DASH (dietary approaches to stop hypertension) diet is considered by many to be an Americanized version of the Mediterranean diet. DASH contains less fish, restricts sodium, and allows the occasional dessert. DASH is sponsored by the National Institutes of Health, has been endorsed by the USDA and the American Heart Association, and has been voted the number one diet by nutritional experts at *U.S. News & World Report* for five years in a row. DASH was originally developed to lower blood pressure and foster heart health, but it has also been proved to be effective for weight loss.

Fasting and Fad Diets

Fasting has been used for thousands of years for religious purposes and to promote health. Advocates of fasting claim that it redirects energy used for digestion to other functions, such as cell repair. While short-term fasts may be safe for some adults, they are not recommended for teens because they can result in nutrient deficiency, fatigue, and other health problems.

Fad diets, which are sometimes called crash diets or celebrity diets, often claim to be based on scientific principles, but they are really modified fasts. For instance, cleanse diets, which instruct the dieter to consume a broth or drink every few hours to remove toxins from the body, work in the short term because they contain very few calories. Juicing, which claims to promote weight loss by loading the body with micronutrients and antioxidants, also works because it limits calories. Despite claims made in commercials and on the web, none of these diets work for long and should be avoided. According to dietitian Ursula Arens, "Crash diets make you feel very unwell and unable to function properly."[49] The online dieting resource FitDay warns, "Most of the weight you will lose [on a fad diet] is just water weight. Once you stop the diet and resume your normal lifestyle, chances are that you will gain the weight back—with a few additional pounds."[50]

> **A study at the University of California–Los Angeles found that up to two-thirds of people who lose weight by dieting eventually regain more weight than they lost.**

Dieting Can Lead to Weight Gain

Many experts caution teenagers about dieting because it can lead to a pattern of weight loss and gain that continues into adulthood. A study at the University of California–Los Angeles found that up to two-thirds of people who lose weight by dieting eventually regain more weight than they lost. This is sometimes referred to as yo-yo dieting or weight cycling—a process of gaining and losing weight through unhealthy weight-loss practices. A ten-year study published in the *Journal of Adolescent Health* found that "specific weight control behaviors used during adolescence that predicted large increases in BMI at 10-year follow-up included skipping meals and reporting eating very little (females and males), use of food substitutes (males), and use of diet pills (females)."[51] In other words, teens who follow unhealthy dieting practices tend to be significantly heavier ten years later.

Eating Disorders

Another problem with dieting is that in some individuals, dieting can cause an unhealthy obsession with weight and food and a pattern of disordered eating (a term that refers to abnormal eating behaviors like compulsive eating and habitual dieting). Disordered eating can lead to serious eating disorders such as anorexia nervosa or bulimia nervosa.

Anorexia is a complex mental disorder in which the person severely restricts the amount of food he or she eats over a long period. Bulimia, which is equally complex, is a mental disorder in which the person regularly binges, or overeats, and then tries to get rid of the food by purging—often by vomiting or using laxatives. Another eating disorder is called eating disorder not otherwise specified, or EDNOS. EDNOS is a catch-all diagnosis that is used when disordered eating becomes dangerous but symptoms do not match anorexia or bulimia. All eating disorders are extremely worrisome; they can cause serious nutritional deficiencies, stunt growth and development, harm internal organs, and lead to death.

Sometimes too much focus on food and weight can turn into an eating disorder before the teen is aware of it. According to eating disorder therapist Josie Tuttle, "It can be really hard for someone in danger of developing an eating disorder to recognize the slippery slope of the diet they're on until they're well on their way down."[52] The Health Experiences Research Group in the United Kingdom interviewed dozens of teens and young adults who struggle with eating disorders and found that, in many cases, their weight-loss efforts morphed into an eating disorder without them realizing it. According to the group's website (which quotes its interviewees), "Once the eating disorder had 'kicked in' in full, people described how things quickly 'spiraled out of control.' Soon they realized they had become engrossed in an obsessive routine of behaviors that 'took on a life of its own.'"[53]

One common myth is that a person must be underweight to have an eating disorder. This is not true; teens at any weight can suffer from these disorders. Nineteen-year-old Jasmine found it difficult to ask for help with her eating disorder after she had regained weight in recovery. "I was struggling," she said, "but I was too worried to talk to people about it because I felt like they'd think I was overreacting because I wasn't underweight." Even medical professionals can misunderstand eating disorders; according to Jasmine, her own doctor "was quite insensitive about the situation just because I looked fine."[54]

> "One common myth is that a person must be underweight to have an eating disorder."

Because eating disorders are so dangerous, teens who show signs of an eating disorder—such as dieting compulsively, purging after meals, doing unhealthy amounts of exercise, or feeling out of control when it comes to food—are urged to talk to a qualified professional regardless of their weight.

Making a Lifestyle Change

Experts agree that teens who want to lose weight should choose a healthy way of eating that they can sustain for the rest of their lives. Some will find it easiest to reduce the level of refined carbs and sugars in their diet; others will do better reducing calories or portion sizes; still others will only need to adopt an active lifestyle to normalize their weight. However, before embarking on any weight-loss program, teens should talk with a doctor or other health care professional to make sure they are getting all the nutrients their bodies need.

Primary Source Quotes*

What Constitutes Healthy Weight Loss?

66 Over the last ten years there have been research studies all over the world that say a low carbohydrate diet is a healthy thing to do. In fact, it is therapeutic for obesity, diabetes, high blood pressure, heartburn, fatty liver—the list goes on and on. 99

—Eric Westman, interviewed by Sam Felton in "063 Debunking Low Carb Myths with Dr. Eric Westman," Smash the Fat, July 16, 2014. http://smashthefat.podbean.com.

Westman is director of the Duke Lifestyle Medicine Clinic at Duke University and coauthor of *The New Atkins Revolution*.

66 If you eat large amounts of fat and protein from animal sources your risk of heart disease or certain cancers may actually increase. 99

—Mayo Clinic staff, "Low-Carb Diet: Can It Help You Lose Weight?," Mayo Clinic, September 20, 2014. www.mayoclinic.org.

The Mayo Clinic is a highly rated hospital and medical research group and the creator of the Mayo Clinic Diet.

Bracketed quotes indicate conflicting positions.

* Editor's Note: While the definition of a primary source can be narrowly or broadly defined, for the purposes of Compact Research, a primary source consists of: 1) results of original research presented by an organization or researcher; 2) eyewitness accounts of events, personal experience, or work experience; 3) first-person editorials offering pundits' opinions; 4) government officials presenting political plans and/or policies; 5) representatives of organizations presenting testimony or policy.

66Avoid what I call edible food-like substances—food that your great grandmother wouldn't recognize. . . . If you eat real food and avoid food-like substances you don't have to worry about calories.**99**

—Michael Pollan, interviewed by Josh Zepps on HuffPost Live, May 13, 2014. http://live.huffingtonpost.com.

Pollan is an author and the director of the Knight Program in Science and Environmental Journalism at the University of California–Berkeley.

66Anyone who has ever lost weight will tell you that it is harder to sustain the weight loss than to lose the weight itself.**99**

—Michael Rosenbaum, *The Weight of the Nation*, directed by Greg Barker. New York: HBO Documentary Films, 2012.

Rosenbaum is a pediatric endocrinologist and a professor of clinical medicine at Columbia University Medical Center.

66The healthiest way to successfully lose weight is to make small changes that will fit into your lifestyle.**99**

—Center for Young Women's Health, "Fad Diets vs. Healthy Weight Management," September 24, 2014. http://youngwomenshealth.org.

The Center for Young Women's Health is a division of Boston Children's Hospital that educates teen girls about health issues.

66All successful diets share three precepts: low sugar, high fiber (which means high micronutrients), and fat and carbohydrate consumed together in the presence of an offsetting amount of fiber.**99**

—Robert Lustig, *Fat Chance: Beating the Odds Against Sugar, Processed Food, Obesity, and Disease*. New York: Penguin, 2013. Kindle edition.

Lustig is a pediatric endocrinologist and a noted lecturer on the dangers of sugar in the diet.

"Figuring out if a teen is overweight can be more complicated than it is for adults. That's because teens are still growing and developing."

—KidsHealth, "When Being Overweight Is a Health Problem," 2015. http://kidshealth.org.

KidsHealth is an online resource for children's health issues created by the Nemours Center for Children's Health Media.

....

"At the age of 15, I decided to change everything. I . . . began eating real foods . . . rather than labeled 'diet' foods."

—Joshua Weissman, *The Slim Palate Paleo Cookbook.* Las Vegas, NV: Victory Belt, 2014. Kindle edition.

Weissman, a teenager who hosts the blog *Slim Palate*, lost more than 100 pounds (45 kg) when he began following a Paleo-style diet.

....

What Constitutes Healthy Weight Loss?

- To lose **1 pound** of body fat, an individual must consume or burn **3,500 fewer calories**.

- In 2015 nutritional experts at *U.S. News & World Report* ranked Weight Watchers as the best diet for weight loss.

- According to a survey of members of the National Weight Control Registry, people who successfully lose weight and maintain weight loss eat breakfast (**78 percent**), watch less than 10 hours of TV per week (**62 percent**), and exercise about an hour a day (**90 percent**).

- Studies conducted at Columbia University Medical Center have found that people who lose weight have a reduction in metabolism and need about **20 percent** fewer calories than people who have never lost weight.

- According to Livestrong.com, teens ate an average of **1 snack** a day in 1980. In 2010 they ate an average of **3 snacks** a day.

- According to the national Youth Risk Behavior Survey, in 2011, **12.2 percent** of high school students reported fasting for 24 hours in the previous 30 days to lose weight or maintain weight loss.

Exercise Helps Speed Weight Loss

A 2014 Canadian study published in *JAMA Pediatrics* found that teens who are dieting to lose weight should do both aerobic and resistance exercise. In the study, over 300 obese teenagers were put on a healthy diet for 22 weeks (with a calorie deficit of 250 calories per day). They were also randomly assigned to one of four groups to test how exercise affected weight loss. The group that did both aerobic exercise (on machines like treadmills) and resistance exercise (using machines or free weights) lost the greatest percentage of body fat and had the greatest decrease in waist circumference after 22 weeks. The group that did not exercise at all saw the smallest reduction in body fat and an insignificant reduction in waist circumference.

Groups	Decline in Body Fat	Decrease in Waist Circumference
Diet plus aerobic and resistance exercise	4.8%	1.6 inches (4.1 cm)
Diet plus aerobic exercise	2.5%	1.2 inches (3 cm)
Diet plus resistance exercise	3.2%	0.8 inches (2 cm)
Diet only	0.6%	Insignificant amount

Source: Nicholas Bakalar, "Teenagers and Weight Loss," *New York Times*, September 24, 2014. http://well.blogs.nytimes.com.

- The Youth Risk Behavior Survey also found that **4.3 percent** of high school students vomited or took laxatives to lose weight in the previous 30 days.

- According to *Time*, people who spend their days sitting typically burn **500 to 1,000 fewer calories** than people who stand most of the day.

The Mediterranean Diet Pyramid

Even though the Mediterranean Diet is a way of eating rather than a calorie-reduction plan, doctors consistently promote it as a tool for healthy weight loss. The diet bases most meals on plant foods, including whole grains, plant protein, vegetables, and olive oil. Red meat and sugar should be eaten sparingly.

Meats & sweets

Poultry, eggs, cheese, & yogurt

Fish & seafood

Fruits, vegetables, grains (mostly whole), olive oil, beans, nuts, legumes, seeds, herbs, & spices

Food Groups	Guidance
Meats and sweets	Less often
Poultry, eggs, cheese, and yogurt	Moderate portions, daily to weekly
Fish and seafood	Often, at least two times a week
Fruits, vegetables, grains (mostly whole), olive oil, beans, nuts, legumes, seeds, herbs, and spices	Base every meal on these foods

Source: Mayo Clinic, "Mediterranean Diet: A Heart-Healthy Eating Plan," June 14, 2013. www.mayoclinic.org.

Increase in Unhealthy Weight-Loss Practices by Boys

A CDC survey of Los Angeles high school students found that the number of boys who engaged in unhealthy methods of losing weight had increased since 2001. Boys were as likely as girls to use diet pills, powders, or liquids without a doctor's advice, and they were nearly as likely to say they purged by vomiting or using laxatives.

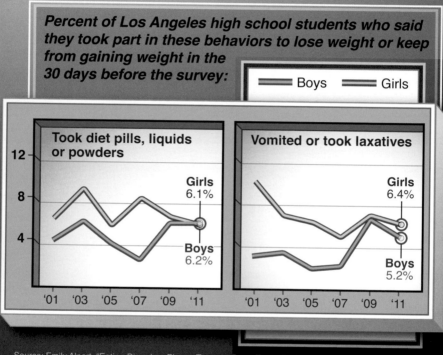

Percent of Los Angeles high school students who said they took part in these behaviors to lose weight or keep from gaining weight in the 30 days before the survey:

Boys — Girls

Took diet pills, liquids or powders

Girls 6.1%
Boys 6.2%

12
8
4

'01 '03 '05 '07 '09 '11

Vomited or took laxatives

Girls 6.4%
Boys 5.2%

'01 '03 '05 '07 '09 '11

Source: Emily Alpert, "Eating Disorders Plague Teenage Boys, Too," *The Viewpoint*, January 30, 2014. http://neviewpoint.com.

- According to a survey by the Schools and Students Health Education Unit in the United Kingdom, more than **60 percent** of **fourteen- and fifteen-year-old girls** said they wanted to lose weight, even though most were not overweight and many were underweight.

- According to the University of Michigan Health System, about **two-thirds** of all new cases of eating disorders are in girls and women who have dieted moderately.

- According to the American Academy of Family Physicians, teens who want to lose weight healthily should limit portion size. A healthy portion of meat should be about the size of a deck of cards, and a portion of rice or pasta should be the size of a fist.

- The National Institutes of Health reports that overweight and obese people who consume diet drinks eat significantly more calories than those who drink sugary beverages.

Key People and Advocacy Groups

American Society for Nutrition: A lobbying group that advocates for improved nutrition research.

Peter Attia: A surgeon and the cofounder of the research organization Nutrition Science Initiative. His blog, *The Eating Academy*, explores how the science of low-carbohydrate eating impacts athletic performance.

T. Colin Campbell: A professor of biochemistry at Cornell University who specializes in the effect of nutrition on health and advocates for a low-fat, plant-based diet.

David Kessler: Former FDA commissioner and dean of Yale and University of California–San Francisco medical schools, Kessler is the author of *The End of Overeating*, which implicates the food industry in the obesity epidemic.

Robert Lustig: A pediatric endocrinologist and professor of clinical pediatrics at the University of California–San Francisco. Lustig is a noted lecturer on the dangers of sugar in the diet.

National Alliance for Nutrition and Activity: A lobbying group that advocates policies and programs to promote healthy eating and physical activity.

National Collaborative on Child Obesity Research: An organization that works to support, improve, and facilitate research into child obesity.

Miriam Nelson: Director of the John Hancock Research Center on Physical Activity, Nutrition, and Obesity Prevention at Tufts University,

Nelson is the award-winning author of the Strong Women series of books that teach women how to use exercise to improve health.

Marion Nestle: A noted nutritionist and professor of nutrition at New York University, Nestle's books are highly critical of the role of politics in the development of nutritional guidelines.

Michelle Obama: The First Lady of the United States and the creator of the Let's Move campaign to end childhood obesity in a generation.

Jamie Oliver: A celebrity chef noted for his global campaign for better food education and improved school lunches.

Michael Pollan: A noted author and professor of journalism at University of California–Berkley, Pollan is an author and activist critical of the industrial food chain and its effect on health.

President's Council on Fitness, Sports, and Nutrition: A governmental organization that works to promote activity and participation in sports among Americans.

Gary Taubes: An award-winning science writer and a Robert Wood Johnson Foundation investigator in health policy research at the University of California–Berkeley School of Public Health, Taubes is the author of *Good Calories, Bad Calories*, which has sparked renewed interest in low-carbohydrate diets as a treatment for obesity.

Eric Westman: A noted researcher and director of the Duke Lifestyle Medicine Clinic, Westman has gained recognition for his success in treating obesity, diabetes, and other metabolic disorders with a low-carbohydrate diet.

Chronology

1980
The USDA publishes *Dietary Guidelines for Americans* for the first time. The guidelines urge Americans to eat a low-fat diet that includes more fruits, vegetables, and whole grains.

2005
A report published in the *New England Journal of Medicine* projects that for the first time, the current generation of children in America may have shorter life expectancies than their parents, due to the rapid rise in childhood obesity.

1990
Nutrition labels are required on all packaged foods sold in grocery stores.

1994
The Clinton administration limits salt and saturated fat in school lunches.

1980   1990   2000

1991
The largest dietary study in history, the Woman's Health Initiative, is launched. It includes a clinical trial to test whether a low-fat diet prevented heart disease and cancer.

1993
Health advocacy groups call for fast-food chains to stop frying with partially hydrogenated oil after it was discovered that people who ate the highest amounts of trans fats had twice the heart attack risk of those who consumed low amounts.

2001
The US surgeon general issues a Call to Action to fight the rising rates of obesity.

2006
The results of the Woman's Health Initiative show that the women in the study lost an average of 2 pounds (907 g) in eight years and increased their abdominal fat. The study concludes that there was no link between dietary fat and heart disease or cancer.

1992
The USDA publishes the food pyramid.

2007
Gary Taubes publishes *Good Calories, Bad Calories*, which makes the argument that low-fat diets increase the intake of carbohydrates, which is responsible for the obesity epidemic.

2015
The Robert Wood Johnson Foundation announces that it will commit $500 million over the next decade to fund research into childhood obesity.

2009
Dr. Robert Lustig gives a lecture that links sugar consumption to rising obesity rates. It is posted on YouTube and receives more than 5.3 million views over the next five years.

2010
First Lady Michelle Obama starts the Let's Move campaign to end childhood obesity in a generation.

2014
Schools in the United States participating in the National School Lunch Program are required to eliminate junk food from school cafeterias and vending machines.

2010

2008
A study in the *Journal of the American Medical Association* reports that the rate of obesity in the United States has reached 32.2 percent among men, 35.5 percent among women, and 18.1 percent among teenagers.

2012
Students at Wallace High School in Kansas make a YouTube video called *We Are Hungry* protesting new school lunch standards based on the Healthy Hunger-Free Kids Act of 2010. It is viewed more than 1 million times.

2011
The USDA replaces the food pyramid with MyPlate.

2010
An analysis of twenty-one nutrition studies published in the *American Journal of Clinical Nutrition* concludes that there is no relationship between the intake of saturated fat and the incidence of heart disease or stroke.

Related Organizations

Harvard T.H. Chan School of Public Health

677 Huntington Ave.
Boston, MA 02115
phone: (617) 495-1000
website: www.hsph.harvard.edu/nutritionsource/

The Harvard School of Public Health offers a wealth of nutritional information through its website, the Nutrition Source. The site also publishes nutrition news as well as information about its nutritional guidelines, the Healthy Eating Plate.

Healthcorps

75 Broad St., 24th Floor
New York, NY 10004
phone: (212) 742-2875
e-mail: info@healthcorps.org • website: http://healthcorps.org

Healthcorps works to implement in-school programs that inspire teens to make healthier food choices. Its website offers educational articles and videos on nutrition and fitness. Healthcorps was founded by Dr. Mehmet Oz.

Kids Eat Right

Academy of Nutrition and Dietetics Foundation
120 S. Riverside Pl., Suite 2000
Chicago, IL 60606-6995
phone: (800) 877-1600
website: www.eatright.org

The Kids Eat Right campaign is a program created by the Academy of Nutrition and Dietetics that supports projects and programs that address childhood obesity and nutrition. Its website contains information for teens, including articles, tips, recipes, videos, and links to resources.

Let's Move

website: www.letsmove.gov

Let's Move is an initiative launched by Michelle Obama to solve childhood obesity that works to educate parents and children about obesity and foster healthy environments that encourage healthy choices. Its website contains information about ways to combat obesity through nutrition and physical activity and includes links to information from the White House Task Force on Childhood Obesity and various articles and fact sheets.

National Federation of State High School Associations Learning Center

PO Box 690
Indianapolis, IN 46206
phone: (317) 972-6900
website: http://nfhslearn.com

The National Federation of State High School Associations Learning Center offers information and training in high school sports issues, including sports medicine and nutrition. It offers a free course on sports nutrition targeted to athletes, parents, and coaches that contains downloadable resources.

Nutrition.gov

National Agricultural Library
Food and Nutrition Information Center
Nutrition.gov Staff
10301 Baltimore Ave.
Beltsville, MD 20705-2351
e-mail: nginbox@ars.usda.gov • website: www.nutrition.gov

Nutrition.gov provides access to food and nutrition information from across the federal government, acting as a gateway to information about healthy eating, dietary supplements, and fitness. The site contains detailed nutrition information for teens.

Nutrition Science Initiative

6020 Cornerstone Ct. W., Suite 240
San Diego, CA 92121
phone: (858) 914-5400
e-mail: info@nusi.org • website: http://nusi.org

The Nutrition Science Initiative is a research organization dedicated to improving the quality of nutrition and obesity research by designing and funding independent research studies. Its website summarizes and links to nutrition and obesity research and details current studies.

Obesity Action Coalition

4511 N. Himes Ave., Suite 250
Tampa, FL 33614
phone: (800) 717-3117
website: www.obesityaction.org

The Obesity Action Coalition is an advocacy organization for people affected by obesity. Its website contains general education information as well as specific information about childhood obesity, obesity treatments, and weight bias and stigma.

Palo Alto Medical Foundation

2350 El Camino Real
Mountain View, CA 94040
phone: (650) 691-6149
website: www.pamf.org

The Palo Alto Medical Foundation has a teen health section on its website that offers comprehensive nutrition and fitness information, including a nutritional analysis tool and information about sports nutrition and weight loss. Some of the information provided is written by teens and reviewed by medical professionals.

US Department of Agriculture Center for Nutrition Policy and Promotion

3101 Park Center Dr., 10th Floor
Alexandria, VA 22302-1594
website: www.cnpp.usda.gov

The Center for Nutrition Policy and Promotion's website contains up-to-date nutrition information for all age groups. The center also publishes the *Dietary Guidelines for Americans*, which are due to be updated in 2015. The website also contains an "Ask the Expert" automated customer support–system feature.

For Further Research

Books
Anita Bean, *Anita Bean's Sports Nutrition for Young Athletes*. London: Bloomsbury, 2013.

Suzanne Girard Eberle, *Endurance Sports Nutrition*, 3rd ed. Champaign, IL: Human Kinetics, 2013.

David Kessler, *Your Food Is Fooling You: How Your Brain Is Hijacked by Sugar, Fat, and Salt*. New York: Roaring Brook, 2013.

Robert Lustig, *Fat Chance: Beating the Odds Against Sugar, Processed Food, Obesity, and Disease*. New York: Penguin Group, 2013.

Michael Moss, *Salt Sugar Fat: How the Food Giants Hooked Us*. New York: Random House, 2013.

Marion Nestle and Malden Nesheim, *Why Calories Count*. Berkeley: University of California Press, 2012.

Gary Taubes, *Why We Get Fat and What to Do About It*. New York: Knopf Doubleday, 2011.

Nina Teichoiz, *The Big Fat Surprise*. New York: Simon & Shuster, 2014.

Periodicals
Mark Bittman, "How to Eat Now," *Time*, October 20, 2014.

Ezekiel Emanuel and Andrew Steinmetz, "Finally, Some Optimism About Obesity," *New York Times*, May 4, 2014.

Roberto Ferdman, "How the American Diet Has Failed," *Washington Post*, June 18, 2014.

John Horgan, "Chewing the Fat with Diet Journalist Gary Taubes," *Scientific American*, October 7, 2014.

Julie Kaiser, "Yo-Yo Dieting Among Teens Has Long-Term Effects," *Springfield (IL) State Journal-Register*, February 27, 2012.

Molly Kimball, "Sports Nutrition: Fueling the Student Athlete," *New Orleans Times-Picayune*, September 16, 2014.

David S. Ludwig and Mark I. Friedman, "Always Hungry? Here's Why," *New York Times*, May 16, 2014.

Anahad O'Connor, "A Call for a Low-Carb Diet That Embraces Fat," *New York Times*, September 1, 2014.

Jacques Peretti, "Why Our Food Is Making Us Fat," *Guardian* (London), June 11, 2012.

Gretchen Reynolds, "Dieting vs. Exercise for Weight Loss," *New York Times*, August 1, 2012.

Bonnie Taub-Dix, "Wrestling with Their Weight . . . Literally," *U.S. News & World Report*, September 28, 2012.

Gary Taubes, "What Really Makes Us Fat," *New York Times*, June 30, 2012.

U.S. News & World Report, "The Best Diets of 2015," January 6, 2015.

Internet Sources

"A Teenager's Nutritional Needs," American Academy of Pediatrics, March 28, 2014. www.healthychildren.org/English/ages-stages/teen/nutrition/Pages/A-Teenagers-Nutritional-Needs.aspx.

Robert Lustig, "Sugar—the Elephant in the Kitchen," lecture given at TEDxBermuda, 2013. www.youtube.com/watch?v=gmC4Rm5cpOI.

Ron Maughan and Louise Burke, *Nutrition for Athletes*, International Olympic Committee, April 2012. www.olympic.org/Documents/Reports/EN/en_report_833.pdf.

Sports Nutrition (training course), National Federation of State High School Associations Learning Center, 2014. https://nfhslearn.com/welcome.

Eric Westman, "The Science Behind Low Carb High Fat," lecture presented at the Central Coast Nutrition Conference, San Luis Obispo, California, June 24, 2014. www.youtube.com/watch?v=SCGDAwp-y0o.

Source Notes

Overview

1. Quoted in Jania Matthews, "Americans Find Doing Their Own Taxes Simpler than Improving Diet and Health," Food Insight, May 22, 2012. www.foodinsight.org.
2. Christina Warinner, "Debunking the Paleo Diet," lecture, TEDxOU, February 12, 2013.
3. Nina Teicholz, *The Big Fat Surprise*. New York: Simon & Shuster, 2014. Kindle edition.
4. Anahad O'Connor, "Myths Surrounding Breakfast and Weight," *Well* (blog), *New York Times*, September 10, 2013. http://well.blogs.nytimes.com.
5. Quoted in CRC Health Group, "Are Wrestlers at Increased Risk for Developing Eating Disorders?," *CRC Health Group Blog*, March 6, 2012. http://blog.crchealth.com.
6. Eric Westman, "The Science Behind Low Carb High Fat," lecture presented at the Central Coast Nutrition Conference, San Luis Obispo, California, June 24, 2014.

How Important Is Nutrition for Teens?

7. Centre for Adolescent Health, "Food for Teenagers," Raising Children Network, March 13, 2013. http://raisingchildren.net.au.
8. Quoted in American Academy of Pediatrics, "A Teenager's Nutritional Needs," March 28, 2014. www.healthychildren.org.
9. Victoria Drake, "Micronutrient Requirements of Adolescents Ages 14 to 18 Years," Linus Pauling Institute, Oregon State University, July 2012. http://lpi.oregonstate.edu.
10. K. Aleisha Fetters, "15 Signs You May Have an Iron Deficiency," Health.com, 2015. www.health.com.
11. Harvard School of Public Health, "Food Pyramids and Plates: What Should You Really Eat?," 2015. www.hsph.harvard.edu.
12. National Institutes of Health, "Calcium," November 21, 2013. http://ods.od.nih.gov.
13. Harvard School of Public Health, "Healthy Eating Plate vs. USDA's MyPlate," 2015. www.hsph.harvard.edu.
14. George Zaidan, "What Is Fat?," *Huffington Post*, August 18, 2013. www.huffingtonpost.com.
15. Harvard School of Public Health, "Fats and Cholesterol," 2015. www.hsph.harvard.edu.
16. Harvard School of Public Health, "The Problem with Potatoes," 2015. www.hsph.harvard.edu.

How Can Teen Athletes Improve Performance Through Diet and Nutrition?

17. Molly Kimball, "Sports Nutrition: Fueling the Student Athlete," *New Orleans Times-Picayune*, September 16, 2014. www.nola.com.
18. American Academy of Family Physicians, "Nutrition for Athletes," September 2011. http://familydoctor.org.
19. Luis E. Palacio, "Nutrition for the Female Athlete," Medscape, May 28, 2013. http://reference.medscape.com.
20. Diane Lynn, "High School Athletes & Nutrition," Livestrong.com, January 28, 2015. www.livestrong.com.

21. Mick Koester, Sports Nutrition (training course), National Federation of State High School Associations Learning Center, 2014. https://nfhslearn.com.
22. Brown University, "Sports Nutrition." www.brown.edu.
23. Quoted in Medical News Today, "How Much Sugar Is in Your Food?," June 16, 2014. www.medicalnewstoday.com.
24. Meredith Melnick, "The Sneaky Sugar in Your Energy Bars," *Huffington Post*, October 24, 2013. www.huffingtonpost.com.
25. Densie Webb, "The Truth About Energy Drinks," *Today's Dietitian*, October 2013. www.todaysdietitian.com.
26. Plataforma SINC, "Energy Drinks Cause Insomnia, Nervousness in Athletes," *ScienceDaily*, October 2, 2014. www.sciencedaily.com.
27. New Health Guide, "Are Monster Energy Drinks Bad for You?," 2014. www.newhealthguide.org.
28. Brown University, "Sports Nutrition."
29. Brown University, "Sports Nutrition."
30. Quoted in Bonnie Taub-Dix, "Wrestling with Their Weight . . . Literally," *U.S. News & World Report*, September 28, 2012. http://health.usnews.com.
31. Quoted in Taub-Dix, "Wrestling with Their Weight . . . Literally."
32. Jorunn Sundgot-Borgen et al., "How to Minimize the Health Risks to Athletes Who Compete in Weight-Sensitive Sports," *British Journal of Sports Medicine*, November 1, 2013, p. 1014.

Why Are More Teens Overweight Today?

33. Rebecca Puhl, "Child Obesity and Stigma," Obesity Action Coalition, 2015. www.obesityaction.org.
34. Quoted in Joanne Barker, "What's Making Me Fat? What Can I Do?," WebMD, January 11, 2012. http://fit.webmd.com.
35. Quoted in Sabrina Tavernise, "Children in U.S. Are Eating Fewer Calories, Study Finds," *New York Times*, February 21, 2013. www.nytimes.com.
36. Quoted in Robert Wood Johnson Foundation, "Consumers Underestimate Calories in Fast-Food Meals; Teens Do So by as Much as 34 Percent," May 23, 2013. www.rwjf.org.
37. Lisa M. Powell and Binh T. Nguyen, "Fast-Food and Full-Service Restaurant Consumption Among Children and Adolescents: Impacts on Energy, Beverage and Nutrient Intake," *JAMA Pediatrics*, January 2013. www.ncbi.nlm.nih.gov.
38. David Kessler, *Your Food Is Fooling You: How Your Brain Is Hijacked by Sugar, Fat, and Salt*. New York: Roaring Brook, 2013. Kindle edition.
39. Kessler, *Your Food Is Fooling You*.
40. Kessler, *Your Food Is Fooling You*.
41. Kessler, *Your Food Is Fooling You*.
42. Robert Lustig, *Fat Chance: Beating the Odds Against Sugar, Processed Food, Obesity, and Disease*. New York: Penguin Group, 2013. Kindle edition.
43. Robert Lustig, interviewed by Alec Baldwin in *Here's the Thing*, podcast, WNYC, July 2, 2012. www.wnyc.org.

What Constitutes Healthy Weight Loss?

44. Quoted in Anahad O'Connor, "A Call for a Low-Carb Diet That Embraces Fat," *New York Times*, September 1, 2014. www.nytimes.com.

45. Mayo Clinic, "Weight Loss: What Are the Options?," June 22, 2012. www.mayoclinic. org.

46. Westman, "The Science Behind Low Carb High Fat."

47. Quoted in Melissa Joulwan, "Paleo Nutrition for Teens," *The Clothes Make the Girl* (blog), February 19, 2014. http://theclothesmakethegirl.com.

48. *U.S. News & World Report*, "Mediterranean Diet Overview," January 5, 2015. http:// health.usnews.com.

49. Quoted in NHS Choices, "How to Diet," September 12, 2013. www.nhs.uk.

50. FitDay, "4 Reasons Why You Should Avoid Fad Diets," 2013. www.fitday.com.

51. Quoted in Julie Kaiser, "Yo-Yo Dieting Among Teens Has Long-Term Effects," *Springfield (IL) State Journal-Register*, February 27, 2012. www.sj-r.com.

52. Josie Tuttle, "The Thin Line Between Diet and Eating Disorder," *Good Therapy* (blog), August 26, 2011. www.goodtherapy.org.

53. Health Experiences Research Group, "The Beginning of an Eating Disorder," HealthTalk.org, 2014. www.healthtalk.org.

54. Quoted in Health Experiences Research Group, "Myths About Eating Disorders," HealthTalk.org, 2014. www.healthtalk.org.

List of Illustrations

Index

Note: Boldface page numbers indicate illustrations.

About the Author

Christine Wilcox writes fiction and nonfiction for young adults and adults. She has worked as an editor, an instructional designer, and a writing instructor. She lives in Richmond, Virginia, with her husband, David, and her son, Doug.